Desdemona,
Lady Macbeth,
and Cleopatra

Desdemona, Lady Macbeth, and Cleopatra

Tragic Women in Shakespeare's Plays

Ana Maribel Moreno G.

DESDEMONA, LADY MACBETH, AND CLEOPATRA
TRAGIC WOMEN IN SHAKESPEARE'S PLAYS

iUniverse books may be ordered through booksellers or by contacting:

*iUniverse
1663 Liberty Drive
Bloomington, IN 47403
www.iuniverse.com
1-800-Authors (1-800-288-4677)*

*Because of the dynamic nature of the Internet, any web addresses or
links contained in this book may have changed since publication and
may no longer be valid. The views expressed in this work are solely those
of the author and do not necessarily reflect the views of the publisher,
and the publisher hereby disclaims any responsibility for them.*

*Any people depicted in stock imagery provided by Thinkstock are
models, and such images are being used for illustrative purposes only.
Certain stock imagery © Thinkstock.*

*ISBN: 978-1-4917-6600-2 (sc)
ISBN: 978-1-4917-6599-9 (e)*

Library of Congress Control Number: 2015911529

Print information available on the last page.

iUniverse rev. date: 10/02/2015

With love to my mother,
Thelma J. Guillén de Moreno

Acknowledgments

Thanks, God, for giving me the opportunity to fulfill this dream.

I wish to give my deepest gratitude to my professor, Dr. Colomba Luque de Pérez, who guided me in literary analysis and Shakespeare's plays.

Contents

Shakespeare is tangible,
immortal and universal.

Introduction

For many years we have read and enjoyed Shakespeare's plays. In this work, we are going to analyze three of his most important female characters: Desdemona in *Othello, The Moor of Venice*; Lady Macbeth in *Macbeth;* and Cleopatra in *Antony and Cleopatra*. We also want to follow the chronological order in which the three plays were written to better understand how Shakespeare was increasing, improving, and magnifying the emotions and reactions of the characters with regard to their expressions of deep passion.

During the last five decades, we have heard, seen, and analyzed a lot about women's liberation; however, we will explore the examples of women's liberation we can find in Desdemona, Lady Macbeth, and Cleopatra. These three women together represent all the facts and decisive actions a woman of our times needs to know to feel liberated. But this work has to do not only with feminism but also with gender and genre, addressing how women can behave in different situations and how their behavior can carry them to their deaths, thus transforming them into tragic women.

In *Othello,* we will find the young, beautiful, white, socially important, and rich girl Desdemona, who decided to marry a middle-aged, black Moor, Othello. Desdemona is what we can call a girl out of her time because it still is not easy for many people, even in our days, to accept a marriage between a black and a white person. We can imagine the force of the emotions in her father, as well as the reaction of the audience in the theater. Her actions at the beginning of the story, and the fact that her father was no longer with his inexperienced child, were the principal causes of her tragic death.

In *Macbeth,* we will find and analyze Lady Macbeth. She is a different kind of character. She represents the bad and dark emotions, the deep thoughts of women. The play is about ambition, and Lady Macbeth is the voice of that ambition. She is a clear example of a domestic woman's domination. She plays a very important role in the life of her husband, and we will find out how her fatal support carries them off to their inevitable, tragic end.

The last chapter will be dedicated to Cleopatra, the most famous woman, queen, and ruler in Shakespeare's works. She was an outstanding and beautiful queen centuries before Shakespeare decided to write *Antony and Cleopatra*. But here we will try to understand her reasons, not only as a woman and a mother but also as a queen fatally in love with the right person for her but at a wrong moment for others.

The other purpose of this work is to analyze these strong female characters in the no-less-intensive plays. Most of the time, in the majority of the existing critical interpretations, the writers offer extensive and deep analyses of the principal male characters, but very few of them talk about the female characters with the same or similar intensity.

We must remember that women did not have a legal status during Shakespeare's time. They were not allowed public or private autonomy. Men controlled society beginning with the family. English society functioned on a so-called system of patriarchy and hierarchy, which was guided by Ptolemy's theory: God existed at the top and was followed by the angels, men, women, animals, plants, and rocks. If all women were thought to exist below all men, we can easily imagine the kind of confusion that was created when Elizabeth I became the queen of England. Nonetheless, an understanding of Ptolemy's concept should be useful for those who begin to study Shakespeare.

This system of patriarchy was accompanied by the practice of primogeniture, a system of inheritance that passed the whole family's wealth to the first male child. Thus, women did not inherit their families' fortunes and nobility titles. Only in some cases, in the absence of a male child, could some women inherit, and this was the case of Elizabeth I. Once the woman got married, she lost all of her limited legal rights, including the right to inherit, to own property, and to sign contracts. Furthermore, women did not go to school and could not enter certain professions, including acting. Women were relegated to their homes.

Chapter 1

Desdemona in Shakespeare's *Othello*

1.1 Literary Background of the Play

The purpose of this chapter is to analyze the character of Desdemona as a woman of her time. We will try to understand the reasons for her behavior in the play.

We are quite clear that Shakespeare's works cannot be called original. From the titles of most of them, we can easily and rapidly conclude that they were copied from other sources or that he simply wrote about the English kings, the English monarchy, and the wars they fought to keep their lands and their thrones.

The story of *Othello, The Moor of Venice* was probably taken from Giraldi Cinthio's

Hecatommithi (1565). The work of Cinthio consists of short stories concerning the theme of marriage. First, he wrote an introduction including ten stories, and following that he presented ten *decades*, each consisting of ten stories or novellas. In writing *Othello*, Shakespeare used the seventh novella of the third decade. In this decade, all the stories were about marital infidelities, and it is precisely in that seventh novella that a husband seeks revenge on his wife because of a supposed infidelity, culminating in her accidental death (Maurer, 19).

As we can see, this summary of one of Cinthio's novellas seems to be the basis for Shakespeare's *Othello*. They are alike in that the husband in Cinthio's work is a Moor, "a very *gallant man*, who was *personally valiant* and had *given proof in warfare* of great prudence and skilful energy." In Cinthio's work, the name of the Moor is never mentioned, but the name of his wife is Disdemona. This is the most convincing reason to believe that Shakespeare's source is, no doubt, Cinthio's book. Cinthio's story also mentions "an Ensign unnamed," but of "the most scoundrelly nature in the world," and his wife is a very good friend of Disdemona. In *Hecatommithi,* we also find a character named Corporal with whom the Moor thinks Disdemona has had an affair. The story of Cinthio also includes some circumstantial evidence used by Shakespeare in *Othello*, such as the handkerchief and the "ocular proof" demanded by Othello.

However, Shakespeare makes many important changes from Cinthio's novella, creating the psychological masterpiece we now study and that has been enjoyed and has held readers spellbound through centuries. Shakespeare develops and gives more action to the Moor and to the ensign in his play. They are forceful and complex, and they are dynamic human beings governed by desires, with both rational and irrational thoughts.

Another important change that Shakespeare completes in *Othello* is the death of Desdemona. Cinthio's novella also insinuates the brutal slaying of Disdemona by the ensign, who is in love with her and who is working as an extension of the Moor. Almost at the end of the source story, we can see the Moor and the ensign planning an elaborate cover-up of their crime (19). In *Hecatommithi,* the Moor's epiphany is through divine intervention, not through his own powers, as is the case in Shakespeare's *Othello*.

Kate Maurer presents the following summary of the climax of *Hecatommithi:*

> In Cinthio's work, God intervenes and creates such a longing for Disdemona in the Moor that he is pushed to the realization of the Ensign's manipulation. In revenge for the wrongs the Ensign has done, the Moor demotes him, which leads to a volatile feud between the two of them. In the end, the Moor is framed for Disdemona's murder by the Ensign and is taken to Venice and tortured under the pretense of gaining information. Ultimately, the Moor is exiled and then mysteriously slain by one of Disdemona's relatives "as he richly deserved," according to Cinthio. The Ensign, too, meets a torturous end, and Cinthio explains all as "God aveng(ing) the innocence of Disdemona." (20)

How Shakespeare could have known about Cinthio's novellas is still a matter of discussion among critics. Some of them suggest he read them in Italian or in a

French or Spanish translation. Maurer points out that the earliest English translation of *Hecatommithi* that survives is from the year 1753. Other scholars say that maybe a real-life event influenced Shakespeare to write *Othello*. Charles Boyce said in 1565, an Italian serving the French government was diverted from a diplomatic mission by false reports of his wife's infidelity, circulated by his enemies. Upon his return home, the husband was satisfied with the wife's denials but strangled her anyway "in the name of honour" (20).

1.2 Desdemona as a Woman

All cultures have their own legends or myths regarding the first human beings, gods, or demigods giving life to the rest of us. According to the Cherokee myth of creation, the first human beings were a brother and sister. In other cultures, like the Aztec, the first life-givers were the sun and the moon; for the Chinese, it was the yin and yang; for Christians, it is Adam and Eve. But all of them have the duality of masculine and feminine figures as beginners of what we know as human beings. That is why we cannot separate the relationship of couples in the work of the bard. But it is also true that some women are different, outstanding, or assigned a more important role. And Shakespeare presented us with some characters representing very strong women, like Cleopatra and Lady Macbeth; others with less power, like Octavia and Calpurnia; and others who are young, weak, and not outstanding, like Ophelia and Juliet. There are also witches, fairies, lovers, and so on. But all these women, regardless of their status or way of living, love their husbands.

If we analyze Desdemona's first line in *Othello*, we understand her nature as the daughter of Brabantio and how it influences the conversations of her father with the duke in the Senate. When she enters the stage the first time, she says,

My noble father. (1.3.180)

These three words denote a very important and crucial connection of feelings between Desdemona and her father. *My* means "possession" in all ways. Since language has a dramatic effect in the play, it has an impact on us, and just as Shakespeare captures our attention nowadays, we can presume that these effects were achieved also in Shakespeare's times. In addition,

Othello is a play of possession: Cyprus is a colony possessed by Venetia; the Turks want to possess Cyprus; Desdemona is the daughter of the widower Brabantio, who thinks that she is his possession; and Desdemona, in saying "my ... father," refers to possession too. Father and daughter are one for the other because they are alone in this world, and they need each other to survive. According to Mowat and Werstine, there is also a trinity of ownership in the play—Othello is the owner of the situation, Desdemona is what he possesses, and Iago is there to be sure that Othello will not recognize Desdemona's imperfection.

The second word, *noble*, implies the social status of Desdemona and her father in the gentle and royal city of Venice. They are noble not because they belong to the duke's family but because her father is a venerable senator of Venice, a city in its golden days, which included the time when *Othello* was originally performed. Venice was the greatest commercial republic in Europe during those days. It was a civilized and democratic city built on water and on the wealth that came by water. Brabantio is an honest, loyal, courageous, and impulsive man; a respectable and considerable man in the republic; and a man respected by the duke himself, which is proven when the duke says to Brabantio,

> Welcome, gentle signior;
> We lack your counsel
> and your help tonight. (1.30.50–51)

For all these reasons, Brabantio is a "noble" man respected by the Venetian people, and his daughter knows it very well. In the third of the three words of Desdemona's first line, we find the resonant *father*. We can analyze and understand this word in many senses, but perhaps the most important is the biblical implication. Since Desdemona, as most of the Venetian citizens, is a Christian, we can suppose that the word has a very special meaning for her. The word means and refers to our "Lord Father," the creator of everything on earth.

The word *father* means "creator," "progenitor," and "the possessor of sons and daughters," and this is the way many cultures and human groups around the world understand it. From ancient times to modern times, the roles of fathers and their children have changed in some cultures, and this is the first conflict we find in analyzing

Othello. The main family problem when this story begins is that Brabantio is surprised in the middle of the night when Iago decides to go with Roderigo to tell him about the marriage of Desdemona and the Moor. Maybe if he had known about the intentions of Desdemona and Othello before they got married, it could be supposed that Brabantio could have prevented the marriage, as many other fathers have done in such cases.

However, the first lines that Brabantio delivers in the play reveal that his relationship with Desdemona is not entirely close. Kate Maurer says, "Brabantio clearly views his daughter as a piece of property—no more or less than a vase, rug or a piece of art—and he compares her marriage as a robbery because he is missing a valuable possession." In the case of Desdemona, we have a young woman whose mother is dead, and because of this she lives alone with her father. This fact is one of Desdemona's main problems within the play—since her mother is not alive, she is ruled completely by her father, as she says,

> To you I am bound for life and education;
> My life and education both to learn me

> How to respect you. You are lord of all
> my duty (1.3.181–183)

She is a kind of possession to her father, she belongs to him, and logically she must be obedient to him. We should analyze here Desdemona as a daughter more than Desdemona as a woman because at her age (she was probably younger than eighteen), she must demonstrate strict submission to her father. However, she decides to leave her father and secretly marry the Moor. This represents the center of this tragedy because the Venetian girl and her love bring destruction and mess up their lives by violating the system and regulations of the community to which they belong, a society in which loyalty and family are the priorities (Watts, 13).

Some recent scholars have argued that Desdemona is more complex as a character than the audiences would have believed in Shakespeare's time. Modern critics analyze Desdemona's as a complicated nature. When she stands up before the Venetian senate, she shows equanimity; she speaks like a mature woman, not like the young woman she was. She convinces the council to allow her to accompany her husband, Othello, to

Cyprus. Desdemona is a woman motivated by her passions. She is concerned about her actions but not because of what they represent to her father and to the traditional society of Venice. She is concerned because she is unwilling to let that which she desires slip through her fingers.

The way Desdemona faces the senate—speaking, acting, and defending her desires, making her dreams a reality—probably made a great impact on the audiences in the times of Shakespeare. She is not a first-class woman; she is not part of the duke's family. Her community relegates her to a second-class status.

Desdemona is the daughter of a venerable and noble old senator of Venice, but she is able to get away from the significant position to which she belongs. She is docile only at the end of the play; from the very beginning when she enters in act 1, scene 3, in lines 180–250, she speaks firmly, without doubt or hesitation. She is pretty sure of what she wants for her life and is ready to defend her love and her marriage. This part of the play is also important because we see the fights between the domestic environment and the political sphere. They are two distant worlds, but if we examine them closely, they have many realities in common.

Kate Maurer comments,

> In many ways, the smaller domestic sphere, which will be explored throughout the bulk of the play, is in essence a microcosm, reflecting on a smaller scale many of the same struggles faced by the country. (55)

In fact, there are evident tactics and dirty ambushes, strategies and alliances, actual facts and apparent facts, and in this sense we can watch the war move from an international environment to a personal one. For Desdemona, the war does not have the regulation of speed she needs, calling Othello away from his honeymoon and setting up a contrast between the conjugal world of the newlyweds and the political problems of a war. However, it is a story about times of peace, times of domesticity, and the battles that fill life in the domestic, not the military, sphere (55–56).

The indication of the situation's urgency is that the council calls for a session in the middle of the night. The duke has reports about their opponents, the Turks (Ottomites), in war over Cyprus, which is a Venetian colony. The first report indicates that there are 107 galleys (large warships); the second report says 140; and another senator enters and says he has recent news of 200 galleys. The inconsistency of these reports creates a nervous climate for the duke and the senators. And of course the audience reacts nervously as it tries to figure out which is correct. At this point, we realize that the state has a big problem, and we can easily compare it with the internal war of Iago's mission for revenge, which is, in essence, his desire to win over Othello, and to Brabantio's desire for justice to have success over the Moor, just as the duke and the republic of Venice wish to have a victory over the Turks.

Othello's fatal defect is his lack of discernment, his inability to see through his adversaries in the domestic field. He is not able to translate what he knows to be true in one aspect of his life to what he knows to be true in another. All these intricate problems, passions, feelings, desires, and malevolence prepare the audience for an intense play. The first three scenes take place at night, just like the marriage night at Cyprus, as well as the last act. Maybe the author uses this as symbolism to refer to Othello's color or to prepare the audience for a dark, gloomy, sad, and deep drama.

1.3 Desdemona, a Woman in Love

Shakespeare takes us little by little into an understanding that there are many similarities and differences among the characters, places, ways of thinking, and interpretations of the actions and words in the play. There is a dramatic importance in the contrast between the city of Venice and the colony of Cyprus. Venice is a city of great civilization and great wealth, as it is the capital of a rich, famous, and powerful commercial empire and the center of European culture of the time.

On the other hand, Cyprus is a colony conquered by the military officers of Venetia, a place of danger and uncertainty. Salgado and Salgado in their criticism compare Cyprus with the storm around its shores, possibly as a symbol of impulse and passion, to keep in the minds of the audience its difference with the civilized and quiet Venice (14–17).

In the same way, we can compare and differentiate Othello and Desdemona.

Othello, like Cyprus, is surrounded by an uncontrollable storm, far from civilization and help, and under attack by enemies, envy, and malevolence. Desdemona is like Venice—beautiful, modern, and full of life; well educated; and ruled by order—totally the contrary of the tumultuous passions that surround Othello and Cyprus (23).

The first time Othello mentions Desdemona is in act 1, scene 2, line 23.

but that I love gentle Desdemona

And her father says in line 64 of the same scene,

Whether a maid so tender, fair and happy

The first descriptions of Desdemona that we get from her father and her husband tell us clearly the kind of person and the kind of woman she is from the beginning of the story up to the end before her death. She is gentle to everybody, she is tender to her father and of course to her husband, and she is courteous to Emilia as well as to all the people she talks to in the play.

We suppose that during those days people

had almost nothing to do for entertainment except to read, go to the theater for a play or an opera, or listen to the stories of the warriors and travelers. Therefore, when Desdemona begins to hear Othello's stories, stories about far lands and unknown kingdoms, the narration must have been fascinating for her, and Othello says so.

> she loved for the dangers I had passed,
> and I loved her that she did pity them
> (1.3.167–168)

When Desdemona enters in lines 246–257, it is the first time the beautiful Desdemona talks like a woman in love.

> That I love the Moor to live with him ...
> The rites for which I love him are bereft me
> And I a heavy interim shall support
> By his dear absence. Let me go with him. (1.3.246–257)

She reacts as most women would react in that time and in our time too. It is when the duke decides to send Othello immediately to Cyprus that Desdemona rapidly realizes that she "a heavy interim shall support" (1.3.256).

Let's understand the word *heavy* as "sorrowful and tedious." It is such because Desdemona and Othello are a newlywed couple. They have been together just a few hours when they are interrupted by the attendants at midnight, and that is not fair for two persons who have just married. Shakespeare decided to send them all with a storm to the place of war because the storm of their lives and their own personal war is going to start in Cyprus.

When everything is clear and Desdemona convinces the duke that she must go with Othello to Cyprus, the first senator says,

> Adieu, brave Moor, use Desdemona well. (1.3.289)

The verb *use* has the same meaning nowadays as it had during Elizabethan times. The senator was instructing Othello to "use Desdemona" the same way we use a chair, a towel, or anything else. The problem is the way the senator understands their marriage. Maybe he does not believe that they love each other, for the senator cannot accept the love between them because they are such a different couple. However, we see the couple's love when Othello says,

> Come, Desdemona, I have but an hour
> Of love, of worldly matters and direction
> To spend with thee. (1.3.296–298)

For they will part early in the morning, and they have spent a lot of time talking to Brabantio, the duke, and the senator, but now it is time to be together. And as Othello says,

> We must obey time. (1.3.298)

They must make good use of the short period of time they have before departing for Cyprus. At line 284 (1.3), Othello also says,

> I assign my wife

which implies a normal use of the possessive word *my* between a husband and a wife. Even in our times we use "my wife" and "my husband" because our spouses are ours and do not belong to someone else. In the last line, when Othello says,

> My Desdemona (1.3.292)

he means that she is *his* Desdemona, that she does not belong to her father anymore, and he wants to be sure that everybody in Venice—including her father, the duke, and the senators—understand and accept that.

The duke tries to get Desdemona to reconcile with her father, asking her to stay with her father, but of course, she refuses, telling Brabantio openly about her conjugal duties.

The rites for which I love him (1.3.255)

This sentence can have many explanations, but Othello says that it is not "mere sensual appetite" that leads to Desdemona's decision to go to Cyprus with him. He also says that he does not have the "clamorous sexual needs of a young man" (20).

He is certainly confirming that the demands of lovemaking will in no way be allowed to interfere with those of duty. Desdemona has spoken loudly and freely about her love for the Moor, but it seems that her husband is able to put everything aside easily. Maybe Shakespeare is undermining the label, the stereotype of the "black man" as an incarnation of vulgar physical sexuality, as he determines the other principal components of that meanness, brutality, and ugliness.

Salgado and Salgado pointed it out in this respect:

> The noble passion of Othello and Desdemona is no more than the squalid affair between an erring barbarian and a super subtle Venetian, based on nothing more lasting and valuable than an old black man's lust for a young white girl and, on her part, a bored sophisticated perverse yearning for exotic thrills. (21–22)

The perception of these critics is the same as that of many others, that the love and passion between Othello and Desdemona is pure admiration for each other, the elemental forces of human passions always admiring the opposite values, or what we have studied in psychology as the "compensation law."

There is no doubt that Desdemona is in love with Othello, but some characters within the play do not think the same way. Her father thinks that Othello used witchcraft, unnatural powers, and so on to seduce his daughter. Iago thinks that their love "is merely a lust of the blood" (1.3.342) and that "she must change for youth" (1.3.58).

These are bad reasons wrongly and unjustly based on appearances, on what people want the truth to be, or, in the case of Iago, what he wants other people to think or believe. We can find many examples throughout the play, such as when Brabantio says,

> A maiden never bold,
> Of spirit so still and quiet that her motion
> Blush'd at herself, and she on spite of nature (1.3.95–97)

These words clearly mean that Brabantio does not know his daughter's true nature. He believes that the girl who is talking in front of the duke and the senators must be enchanted. And we can add that it is not the same girl at the end of her life.

In act 3, scene 4, we can see that Desdemona and Emilia speak with no point in common. Emilia says that the relationship between husband and wife is clear in terms of appetite and possession.

> Women are food for men, who are only
> the stomachs, and when they are full they belch us. (1.3.97–99)

This metaphor suggests that it is part of the natural order of things, that mankind has been and has thought this way for centuries. But things are changing—women have been changing things, and they must not accept such treatment.

1.4 Desdemona, a Tragic Woman

Desdemona is the tragic woman of the play; she is the subject and object of the purposes of Iago. In act 1, scene 1, some of Iago's lines tell us of his hypocrisy and his false words and phrases.

> whether I in any just term am affined
> I love the Moor. (1.1.38–39)

A person who is able to say this when in reality he is planning the worst for the person he is talking about must be someone who is corrupt inside, is insane, and has a sick soul. He confirms this when he says,

> I will wear my heart upon my sleeve
> For daws to peck at. I am not what I
> am. (1.1.65)

Some lines ahead, he says to Roderigo,

I must show out a flag and sign of love
(1.1.154)

How could Othello and Desdemona discover
Iago's plans if he speaks like a good person
and a good friend?

Shakespeare uses metaphor and symbolism
in some parts of the play. Desdemona
represents the city of Venetia—the civilized,
wealthy, secure, and respectable city—while
Othello represents the black devil, the dark
part of the world. The stranger may be using
magical potions and witchcraft to seduce
the innocent Desdemona. Another symbol
becomes clear when we read that Cassio and
Othello departed for Cyprus in the storm. At
the same time, their lives are in the middle
of an unseen storm that they ignore.

The chidden billow seems to pelt the
clouds;
The wind-shake surge, with high and
monstrous mane, Seems to cast
water on
the burning Bear … and quench the
guards
of th'ever-fixed Pole (1.2.11–15)

This description of the storm while arriving in Cyprus is precisely the setting and background of the atmosphere surrounding their lives, and Shakespeare takes the audience into this scene of high tides, stormy winds, and turbulent emotions through a metaphor that will be actualized in the storm through which Othello and Desdemona move out to get to Cyprus, which was isolated, while they are without help and exposed to all the dangers of the Ottomites—the same condition Desdemona will be in when they reach the island.

Desdemona tells an innocent "lie" to her husband when she says that the handkerchief is not lost, and she misunderstands Othello's reaction—induced and increased by all the intrigues of Iago. She thinks that it must be a state matter. However, Emilia thinks that it must be a "jealous toy" that has affected Othello. If at this point Desdemona had been conscious that she had lost the handkerchief, and if she had said the truth, it would have changed the course of the story, but she ignores the fact that the handkerchief fell down and that Emilia gave it to Iago. The pure, innocent newlywed in love, Desdemona, is unable to think or imagine anything wrong about her husband (47).

When Othello explains the origin of the handkerchief, pointing out its emblematic and special nature, we understand how important this "object" and this "ocular proof" will be for the development of the story. The associations of the handkerchief with marital fidelity, supernatural powers, and a dying mother's gift reinforce the atmosphere of mystery and strangeness around Othello.

Suddenly, Desdemona has a tiny, clarifying thought when Emilia asks,

> Is not this man jealous? (3.4.93)

Desdemona answers,

> I ne'er saw this before
> Sure, there's some wonder in this handkerchief (1.3.94–95)

She does not place too much importance on her own words.

> I am most unhappy in the loss of it. (3.4.96)

This line of Desdemona's is a kind of prediction, but she is still not conscious of it. Iago's plans are getting results in the sense that now Othello is convinced that the handkerchief is a symbol of his wife's honor and of her love for him, and Desdemona realizes that

My lord is not my lord. (3.4.119)

But she does not stop to analyze what she is saying. She should go deep into her own thoughts and her conversations with her husband about their affairs as a couple, but she simply continues worrying about Cassio, taking care of public themes, and ignoring the tempest around her.

Othello has a deep suffering; he is poisoned by the words of Iago. There is increasing desperation between reality and doubt. His mind is completely infected by Iago's dangerous suggestions. Shakespeare gives a wonderful demonstration of the power of language, to create out of "airy nothing" "the forms of things unknown," as he says in another of his famous plays, *A Midsummer Night's Dream*.

Othello no longer has any faculty to see with his eyes or judge with his own mind. Iago is genuinely superior to Othello in an intellectual sense because, at this point, Othello's vision of reality is entirely created out of the words and illustrations that Iago provides. Othello sees and thinks only what Iago wants him to believe, and Desdemona is in the "eye of the storm" as the center of Iago's diabolic plans—but she is totally ignorant of this.

In act 4, scene 2, the greatest emotional distance exists between the lovers, with the ingenuous Desdemona aware of Othello's wild irritation but lacking an understanding of what is happening. This is why she says,

> I understand a fury in your words,
> But not the words. (4.2.32)

To this, Othello compares her with an angel who is going to do something very bad, but Desdemona is not able to analyze his words. Her ignorance is pathetic, and she thinks that he is referring to the war with the Ottomites.

In this same act, we are approaching the fatal end. Othello is angry and almost crazy with jealousy. Desdemona is a little ashamed because she does not understand her husband's attitude. She is trying to be polite. She is acting and speaking like a woman in love when she says,

> My lord, what is your will?

What is your pleasure? (4.2.22–24)

Othello continues verbally attacking her, but she says that she is

Your wife, my lord, your true and loyal wife (4.2.34)

This line is a kind of demand. By this time, Desdemona cannot handle the situation, and her religious formation appears in most of her following entrances. She mentions the words *heaven, Christian*, and *faith,* and she utters some worrying phrases several times in the next dialogues as an intuition that something horrible is over her. She knows that the words of Othello imply terrible suggestions, and the audience may begin to think that Desdemona is about to be murdered.

Desdemona begins to understand her husband's behavior; he has used the word *whore* many times and she is still ignoring the reason, but now she knows that Othello is accusing her of something terrible. But what is all this about? This is the heaviest dialogue between them because both are talking of two different themes; however, the audience knows what is going on, giving great emotion to this part of the play. Desdemona is a very educated and cultured girl of Venice; therefore, she cannot mention the word *whore,* as she says to Iago,

> But never faint my love. I cannot say "whore":
> It does not abhor me now I speak the word (4.2.161)

In this dialogue, Desdemona also asks Iago to help her. She tells him,

> Good friend talk with my husband
> because I do not know
> what is happening to him (4.2.150–153)

This is new proof that Desdemona is simpleminded. She does not have any idea what is happening around her, and of course Iago is very happy because his plans are taking the exact form he has been waiting for.

Desdemona is resolved to please Othello and to trust in the intensity of her love. Othello asks her in front of Lodovico to go to bed, to dismiss Emilia, and to wait for him. She is calm after making this decision as if a great anxiety has been removed. Her mind is moving easily toward childhood memories, love, madness, fatality, and the task of undressing.

The song that Desdemona remembers about her mother's maid is very significant at this point of the story because the maid had died singing it, and we know that Desdemona is soon to be killed. The song is sad, with soft and repeated rhythmic sounds; it has a profoundly calming and relaxing effect and opens the door to the fatal outcome.

Finally, in act 5, scene 2, Desdemona is on her bed, and Othello enters with a light to fulfill his plans. Othello's soliloquy here is full of love for Desdemona. He compares her skin with snow and "monumental alabaster," and he uses magical metaphors with light and life; we can restore light, but we cannot restore life, not even with "Promethean heat" (5.2.1–25)

Desdemona is asleep, but Othello kisses her as if telling her good-bye, as most lovers do. She wakes up, and in their final dialogue, Othello accuses her of infidelity and, for the first time, tells her what he knows about the handkerchief. Desdemona cannot believe what she is hearing. She replies,

Send for the man and ask him (5.2.51)

This tells us why Desdemona hadn't been aware that Othello suspected her of infidelity—the idea is simply unthinkable for her. She really loves her husband, but Othello abuses Desdemona emotionally, psychologically, physically, and verbally, slapping her and calling her a whore many times.

But it is too late. Desdemona's protests of innocence are not enough. She tells him that the only thing she knows is that she loves him and that she has not offended him at any time. The desperate Desdemona begins to implore for her life. First she asks for banishment, but realizing that death is forthcoming, she begs for a pardon through the night, just half an hour, and then just the time to say one prayer. Desdemona asks for mercy, and Othello says, "Amen."

She also says, "Kill me tomorrow, let me live tonight," and he answers, "It is too late." And then he smothers her (5.2.55–85).

Our last hope for Desdemona's survival departs when Othello says, "It is too late."

The Moor touches our empathy as he

considers a world without his rose, his sweet Desdemona, when he tells Emilia,

> O, insupportable! O, heavy hour!
> Methinks it should be now a huge eclipse
> Of sun and moon. (5.2.100–104)

According to Salgado and Salgado, maybe Shakespeare had good reason "to trust the dramatic instinct or experience which led him to devise an ending which is both more powerful and more appropriate" (70).

Othello kills his wife with his own hands, in the same way an artist makes a piece of art. It is the most "drawn-out murder in all Shakespeare's plays and the only time he shows a woman slowly killed by physical violence" (205).

Many authors make suggestions regarding the end of the play. Others ask what could have happened if Desdemona had the right words to speak in those moments—just the exact sentence to prove her innocence. Could she have changed her destiny if she had more time to convince her husband? Since jealousy is the dominant theme for this play, we face a lack of arguments to save

Desdemona. We want her to survive, but this tragedy has psychological contradictions and discrepancies in the duration of time, and that is one reason to think that we cannot have the probability that Desdemona could be saved. Some authors believe that it takes only thirty-six hours from their landing in Cyprus to the end of Desdemona. Others say that the relationship between Iago and Desdemona probably began before Othello's appearance in her life. But this changeability of some characters is common in Elizabethan times in such a way that only by making an icy and intensive psychological analysis of the characters can we find answers to some questions.

As we pointed out before, Desdemona shows weakness at the end of the play. She needs strong statements; she needs to be firm, as when she was in front of the senate. She needs more arguments to defend herself. She needs to move from that bed and ask for some help. But instead of all these actions, she stays in her bed with her confused husband, who is asking her if she has prayed because he is going to kill her. Desdemona is so weak, tired, and confused that she's rather passive when Othello smothers her, and surprisingly, she blames herself for

Othello's physical and emotional abuse. This is the best proof that Desdemona is a tragic victim in this play.

Obedience and loyalty to her husband have been part of the meaning of marriage for Desdemona, and her last words—an acceptance of blame—are wholly characteristic of her. For Salgado and Salgado, the killing of Desdemona is now "not only a stage in Othello's moral decline but an event in the public, external world. As Othello had conceived it, the act had been single and simple, emotionally as well as spiritually and even aesthetically satisfying" (72).

We have to reflect on the vision of tragedy in society where innocence can be dangerous and where it may be guilty. Throughout the play, we try to avoid the extremes of considering Desdemona as totally innocent or entirely guilty, without ever minimizing Othello's portion in her destiny or Iago's unreasonable complicity in bringing all the components to the grotesque end.

Chapter 2

Lady Macbeth in Shakespeare's *Macbeth*

1.1 Literary Background of the Play

Shakespeare probably also found more than one source when writing one of his most famous tragedies, *Macbeth.* According to David Bevington, the story was one of the works of a fourteenth-century priest named John of Fordum and then of a fifteenth-century chronicler named Andrew of Wyntoun. These early sources were compiled by Hector Boece in his *Scotorum Historiae* (1526–1527). Finally, in an edition of 1587, Raphael Holinshed wrote his *Chronicles of England, Scotland, and Ireland,* which was the one used by Shakespeare to write *Macbeth*.

The historical character, who was a king from

1040 to 1057, took the throne of Duncan, killing him in a civil fight between two clans fighting for the empire. However, Macbeth was defeated by the Earl of Northumbria (Siward in *Macbeth*) at Birnam Wood in 1054. The earl was forced to retire, and Macbeth was called to rule for the next three years. After this period, Malcolm killed him. Apparently, Banquo and Fleance were invented by Boece because, at the time Holinshed found it, the story of Macbeth was more fiction than reality.

In the Holinshed story, Duncan assigned Banquo to be Thane of Lochaber and Macbeth, his cousin, to defend Scotland: "first against Macdowald (Macdonwald in *Macbeth*), with his Irish Kerns and galloglasses, and then against Sueno, King of Norway." (Shakespeare fuses these battles into one.) Soon and subsequently, Macbeth and Banquo encounter "three women in strange and wild apparel, resembling creatures of elder world," who predict their futures as in the play. Macbeth and Banquo believed that the three women were the Weird Sisters, some kind of bad fairies, nymphs, or spirits of destiny. However, Macbeth soon became the Thane of Cawdor. But Duncan named his eldest, underage son Malcolm as Prince of

Cumberland and heir to the throne. Macbeth was upset because the law of Scotland said that until the king's son was an adult, the next of kin must be the king, and Macbeth, as his cousin, should have reigned. Macbeth began to plan a way to get the throne, and his very ambitious wife also wanted to be the queen. Banquo and other friends were ready to kill the king at Inverness or at Bothgowanan, not at Macbeth's castle as in the story of Shakespeare.

Malcolm and Donald Bane, the sons of the dead king, ran away to Cumberland, where they would have the protection of Edward the Confessor, King of England, but later Donald Bane went to Ireland.

For ten years, Holinshed's Macbeth was not a tyrant like the character in Shakespeare's play. But the promises of the Weird Sisters were still in the air, which referred to the posterity of his friend Banquo through his sons. Fleance escaped and later found the lineage of the Stuart kings. Bevington says that this genealogy is fictitious.

In the story of Holinshed, we can find also the premonitions of the Weird Sisters that the king was never to fear a man born of woman nor does "any vanquishment till Birnam Wood come to Dunsinane" (100). Macduff went to England to meet Malcolm, but Macbeth's soldiers killed Macduff's wife and children at Fife. Malcolm and Macduff returned to Scotland and defeated Macbeth at Birnam Wood, where their soldiers carried branches before them. Finally Macduff confessed that he was not born of woman because he was "ripped out" of his mother's womb.

Saving some changes, there is no doubt that Shakespeare's *Macbeth* is the same story, but the bard from Stratford also took some fragments of another of Holinshed's stories: *The Murder of the King Duff.* In this case, Shakespeare combined one story with another Holinshed story about someone named Donwald who killed a king named Duff. Other supplementary sources may have been George Buchanan's *Rerum Scoticarum Historia* (1582), King James I's *Daemonology* (1597), John Studley's early seventeenth-century version of Seneca's *Medea,* and Samuel Harnett's *Declaration of Egregious Popish Impostures* (1603), and Shakespeare may have also taken some accounts of famous Scottish trials published around 1590 (102).

Another important detail that is not clear is the year in which Macbeth was written. The version performed in 1606 is different from the First Folio published in 1623, and both differ from the version witnessed by Simon Forman in 1611. Arthur Melville Clark and Dover Wilson believe that the play was written in 1601 because it contained allusions to the Gowrie conspiracy of the previous year. Daniel Amneus has argued for an earlier date, 1599. Amneus also gives us a list of nineteen unsolved problems within the play. According to him, they are due to the cuts and alterations made in 1606 (Muir, 19).

1.2 The Weird Sisters: Supernatural Women

Harold C. Goddard, who wrote a literary criticism about *Macbeth*, thinks that it is a play dedicated "not to the supernatural nor to the blood but to the relation between the two." A modern reader of Shakespeare who does not like the word *supernatural* may substitute the word *unconscious*. *Macbeth* is a play of supernatural representatives and also a play about human passions because its characters have the capacity to be affected by "external agents." Goddard also says,

Hamlet is to Macbeth somewhat as the Ghost is to the Witches. We love and admire Hamlet so much at the beginning that we tend to forget that he is as hot-blooded as the earlier Macbeth when he kills Polonius and the King; cold-blooded as the later Macbeth or Iago when he sends Rosencrantz and Guildenstern to death.

Who are the Weird Sisters? There is not a verse or a single syllable in the play to indicate that they are anything but women. However, almost every verse of the play referring to them implies that they have a close relationship with the Evil One, that they are in intimate contact with the criminal world. "They have received from evil spirits certain supernatural powers, to control the weather, to become invisible, to foresee the future" (Bradley, 27). We are not sure if they are supernatural beings or women who have sold their souls to other supernatural beings. Anyway, there is something mysterious and wonderful about the witches, and that is the tip of inducement to commit a crime.

Some critics have considered that the origin of the witches has been referred to by

Middleton, since two songs from his play *The Witch* are sung in Macbeth. The first is in act 3.

> Come away: Come away:
> Hecate: Hecate, come away
> Hecate I come, I come, I come, I come
> (3.5.32)

And in act 4, we find another.

> Black spirits and white, red spirits and grey,
> Mingle, mingle, mingle, you that mingle may! (4.1.43)

There is a famous paragraph of Charles Lamb's in his *Works,* describing the differences between Middleton's witches and Shakespeare's Weird Sisters.

> Shakespeare's Weird Sisters are creatures to whom man or woman plotting might resort for occasional consultation. Those originate deeds of blood, and begin bad impulses to man. From the moment that their eyes first met Macbeth he is spellbound. That meeting sways his destiny. He can never break the fascination. These witches can hurt the body; those

have power over the soul. They are foul anomalies, of whom we know not whence they are sprung nor whether they have beginning or ending. As they are without human passions they seem to be without human relations. They come with thunder and lighting, and vanish to airy music. This is all we know of them. Except Hecate, they have no names. (55)

The Weird Sisters do not deposit the germs of evil in Macbeth; they have no power over the blameless. They need human passions to exist, and that is what they get in that castle with the Macbeths and the other people around them (Muir, 35).

Some ingredients in the witches' cauldron are associated with the darkest and cruelest elements of human nature: dangerous like the shark; poisonous like the adder; evil like the bat; perverse like the wolf; and diabolic parts like the tooth, the scale, the sting, the maw, the gall, and the entrails. Who are the Weird Sisters? Destiny? Fatality? Three old women from hell? Or something we do not know or even imagine (26–27)?

The witches are the first to enter on stage

with thunder and lightning; they begin to talk only when everything is in silence, and they act as if they are empowered by the noise and disturbance of the storm. Macbeth and Banquo meet the three women "in strange and wild apparel, resembling creatures of elder world" (Bevington, 110). And the three of them mention Macbeth's three future nobility titles. Putting aside the surprise that these messages cause them, Banquo asks him,

> Good sir, why do you start, and seem to fear
> Things that do sound so fair?
> I' th' name of truth,
> Are ye fantastical, or that indeed
> (1.3.151–154)

Then, when Macbeth asks the witches for more explanations about the prophecies, they vanish. About this, Bevington says,

> Herewith the foresaid women vanished immediately out of their sight. This was reputed at the first but some vain fantastical illusion by Macbeth and Banquo ... But afterwards the common opinion was that these women were either the Weird Sisters, that is,

the goddesses of destiny, or else some nymphs or fairies endued with knowledge of prophecy by necromatical science, because everything comes to pass as they had spoken. (110)

Who are the Weird Sisters? Goddard says that the witches in *Macbeth* are perhaps the complete antitypes to peace in Shakespeare. He also says that the witches are incarnations of the death-force, that they are women for sure, or that maybe they are not. Or maybe they are under-women who have regressed beyond the distinctions of sex (28). When Banquo talks to them the first time, he says,

You should be women,
And yet your beards forbid me to interpret
That you are so. (1.3.45–47)

The verses of the three witches greatly encourage and put pressure on Lady Macbeth to commit the murder since she had previously only been thinking about and planning on how to be a queen and to be called "your majesty." To our point of view, the implicit relationship between Lady Macbeth and the witches is very important. They do not need to meet her and to talk with her because she herself invokes them to enter into her heart (112).

> Hie thee hither,
> That I may pour my spirits in thine ear. (1.5.23–24)

Perhaps Lady Macbeth and the second witch have the same guilty thoughts.

> Who can question who poured the suggestion into Lady Macbeth's ear, and helped Macbeth to execute it later? It is the Adam and the Eve story over again, with the Witches in the role of the Serpent. (29)

The witches are the arms and thoughts of Lady Macbeth, or maybe Lady Macbeth is an expansion, an additional cord or thread, of the fourth witch. She can hear them with her senses only, or maybe she is only hearing her inner voices. Her own desires and her ambitions are a kind of mixture with her husband's passions, feelings, and dreams.

1.3 Lady Macbeth as a Woman

There are many differing views about the origin of the play, about the different sources that Shakespeare used, and also about the character of Lady Macbeth. One of the documents that we have of that time, of an early performance of the play, was written by Simon Forman. It is a description of a performance at the Globe in the spring of 1611, and he made reference to the character of Lady Macbeth in the play.

> And mackbeth contrived to kill Duncan,
> & thorowe
> The persuasion of his wife did that
> night Murder the
> Kinge in his own Castle, beinge his
> gueste ...
> Observe Also howe mackbeths quen
> did Rise in the
> Night in her slepe, & walke and talked
> and confessed
> All. & the doctor noted her words.
> (Muir, 16)

The fact is that, as early as 1611, this compositor thought that Lady Macbeth pushed Macbeth to kill Duncan in his own castle, and this is one of the main points we are going to analyze in this work.

The play of *Macbeth* is rich and complex. It transports us from ambition to evil, from obsession for power to death, and we do not know exactly where we are. Shakespeare has to tell us where we are in each scene. Ultimately, we must be in hell because Lady Macbeth has prayed to the murdering spirits. Hell is a state, not a place. The tragedy of *Macbeth* might appear then as a second Fall, with Lady Macbeth as a second Eve (27).

We cannot comment about ambition in *Macbeth* without referring to Lady Macbeth because the play is focused closely on Macbeth and his wife. The relationship between the two is no more than the traditional one between male and female. Again, we have to compare this couple with Adam and Eve, where the man is more rational but shares the sin of his wife. She does not meditate on the consequences of sinful ambition and so becomes tempting to her husband. Both of them fall in an environment of marital complicity and confidence; Lady Macbeth is motivated by ambition for her husband, and in the same way he needs her approbation to carry out the crime.

The play is Shakespeare's most profound exploration of the psychology of malevolence and evil. The process of the play shows us a valiant soldier, Macbeth, who, helped by his wife, represses loyalty, love, and kindness to get the throne. The murder challenges all his powers. He accomplishes the fulfillment of his desires after a long effort and fight—and after coming to the recognition that the throne does not bring shelter.

Lady Macbeth has no idea of the nature of murder at the beginning of the story. She does not think about the "human results" of the murder. She only thinks that by killing Duncan, Macbeth will be the king. She is, therefore, able to bully him into overcoming his fears (Foakes, 11). The assumption of the dominant male role by the woman would bring to the Elizabethan audiences numerous "biblical, medieval, and classical" similitudes on criticizing the triumph of passion over reason.

> Eve choosing for Adam, Noah's wife taking command of the Ark, the Wife of Bath dominating her husband, Venus emasculating Mars. (24)

The moral imagination of Lady Macbeth is different from her husband's. He is always hearing voices, he sees a dagger in the air and the ghost of Banquo, and he hears a voice crying, "Sleep no more."

But Lady Macbeth does not hear or see. The discernment and unreasonable thoughts of Lady Macbeth in facing the crime tell us that something is spiritually corrupt in her. The importance of the moral imagination over the material universe was never expressed in such a way as in *Macbeth.* For Macbeth and Lady Macbeth, "space is forever put in its place" (16).

Shakespeare helps us to understand the nature of Lady Macbeth and the kind of woman she is. In her first entrance on stage, she is reading the letter sent by her husband informing her about the Weird Sisters and about the details of the prophetic future. Lady Macbeth is reading the letter aloud, maybe because she wants to believe the news. Perhaps she is trying to imitate her husband's speech in order to enter into his mind. Maybe she had already read the letter before several times, and the imagery of what is going to happen is easy for the audience and for the reader.

After she finishes reading the letter, a messenger enters and tells her,

The King comes here tonight. (1.5.27)

Now to her, the word *King* means only "Macbeth," her husband, and upon hearing the word *king*, she feels a shock because Duncan is not expected that night in the castle and the third prophecy of the witches is still to be fulfilled. King Duncan's visit was not announced in the letter, yet he is coming. She immediately thinks that the king should be murdered and that, as the Weird Sisters said, Macbeth will be the next king (Russell, 25–27).

In reading the letter, a whole vision comes to Lady Macbeth like a Dante-esque picture. Suddenly, in her first soliloquy, Lady Macbeth reveals a plan. She already has in mind the idea that Macbeth is going to be the king pretty soon and, of course, that she is going to be the queen. The soliloquy includes deep thoughts and dark desires. She invokes the spirits, as if they are always in her presence, as her dearest friends.

> Unsex me here, and fill me,
> from the crown to the toe,
> Top full … (1.5.39–40)

It is the exclamation of a very ambitious woman who is thinking only about power, forgetting her probable religious formation and the transgression of her beliefs. She also says,

> May thick my blood (1.5.41)

This line has a significant implication—maybe her words mean that she wants to have "cold blood" as most murderers have when committing their crimes. She wants to have cold blood to do the murder as she has planned it, and she does not want to suffer remorse or any kind of tension after committing the crime. Regarding this, John Russell says, "The soliloquy is as full of tender feelings as it is of cruelty and very palpable horror" (27).

There are few entries where Lady Macbeth talks like a simple woman, such as when she says in this first soliloquy,

> Come to my woman breast. (1.5.44)

She is still convinced that she is only a simple and mortal woman, but she is also conscious that she needs supernatural help. She is calling the spirits, the night, the murdering ministers, and the smoke of hell; everything must be ready before she takes the murderous knife.

From line 35 to line 70, we see very clearly that Lady Macbeth already has a plan to kill Duncan. When she meets Macbeth for the first time after reading the letter, her salutation reveals that she is completely sure that her husband is

Great Glamis! Worthy Cawdor!
Greater than both … (1.5.53–54)

The last line means that Macbeth will also be the king as the Weird Sisters have said. Macbeth and Lady Macbeth had never talked about the murder before, but it is implicit in their first dialogue as if she can read what Macbeth is thinking.

You face, my thane, is a book. (1.5.60)

As an astute and intelligent woman, Lady Macbeth assumes that her husband is afraid to do what they know must be done by reading each other's thoughts and feelings. There is no doubt that it is an intense and deep dialogue between the couple where "damnation and cruelty are still in their mind with images of violent tempest" (33).

They are totally involved; Lady Macbeth's complete understanding of what is passing within her husband's mind expands and increases their determination to commit the murder. It is Lady Macbeth who receives the king in the castle with words of poisonous honey. She probably kneels low before him. Her first sentence is elegant and stylish, like a ballad or a poem, and its words are simple and almost conventional. Duncan cannot imagine the terrible implications of the false greetings of his hostess, who is carrying him to a death trap (29).

In Macbeth's first soliloquy (1.7.1–28), he enters his first lines with monosyllables. He speaks about haste, the assassination, and bloody instructions. It is clear that Macbeth becomes more rational in this moment when he enumerates the reasons why Duncan should not be murdered, but the lamentable fact is that Lady Macbeth is not listening to him.

In their next dialogue, Lady Macbeth gets angry when she feels a kind of hesitation in her husband's words. She complains, telling him that he is "the man," meaning that he must commit the murder because it is a task for a man, not a woman.

Lady Macbeth makes a very important declaration, in which she says,

> To love the babe that milks me;
> I would, while it was smiling in my face,
> Have plucked my nipple from his boneless gums (1.7.54–57)

She uses precise words to tell us that nothing would make her change what she has decided to do. Murder is in her mind.

Sarah Siddons, an actress who played the role several times, believed that such a tender allusion in the midst of her dreadful language proved that Lady Macbeth "has really felt the maternal yearnings of a mother toward her babe and that she used her very virtues as the means to taunt her husband action." Judi Dench, who played the role in 1976, says that the description of Lady Macbeth's babe was a steady, screwed-up self-desecration (91).

There is nothing clear in the play to indicate whether Lady Macbeth has children or not. However, at line 73, Macbeth says,

> Bring forth men-children only! (1.7.73)

Because of this, Glen Byam Shaw, who directed the play at Stratford-upon-Avon in 1955, believed that Macbeth had had an only son who had died and that Macbeth refers to the sorrow that they still felt over the loss of the babe (Mullin, 26).

At the end of the first act, we do not have any idea of what kind of woman Lady Macbeth was before she received the letter with the news of the meeting of Macbeth with the witches. But it is quite clear that from the very moment that she is reading the letter, she shows us a strong and decisive woman, a woman who is able to support and help her husband in any action. Not only that, but with her very good planning of the murder of Duncan, she convinces her husband immediately.

At the beginning of the second act, with not many words exchanged between them, Lady Macbeth has all the details of the murder in order. But Macbeth doubts now, hesitating when he meets Banquo. He is having strange visions and hallucinations. In his soliloquy at lines 30 to 60, he gives us the first sign that his mind is not clear. Following are some important verses in this respect:

> Is this a dagger which I see before me,
> The handle toward my hand? Come let
> me clutch thee:

> I have thee not, and yet I see thee
> still. ...
> A dagger of the mind, a false creation
> Proceeding from the heat-oppressed
> brain? ...
> And on the blade and dudgeon, gouts
> of blood (2.1.33–46)

We have no doubt that Macbeth is desperate because of the murder they are going to commit. But how is Lady Macbeth? She enters at the beginning of the second scene talking constantly because, as she says, she is not courageous enough to be in silence. She wants to be queen at any price, but she is becoming unreasonable and now what she wants most is to see the prophecies of the witches fulfilled. She also hears an owl's cry but thinks that maybe it is only in her mind.

In this scene is the only time in the whole play when Lady Macbeth calls Macbeth "husband." At line 13, Lady Macbeth greets him when he arrives and says,

> My father as he slept, I had done't.—
> My husband? (2.2.13)

This line is very important because, from here up to line 57, they have a unique conversation as a married couple. Macbeth is worried about what they are doing, but Lady Macbeth is resolute and supportive. Both are frightened, but she seems to be in command. The words of the dialogue are whispered, and there are silences after the pauses. This is the most nervous and strongest conversation between them. It is a quiet and tense scene because instead of there being time to express satisfaction, Macbeth is tormented by pity and fear, but Lady Macbeth consoles him, saying,

Consider it not so deeply. (2.2.30)

They both are afraid of the bloody dagger they can see now with horror, but Lady Macbeth tries to calm herself and her husband when she says,

Give me the daggers. The sleeping and the dead
Are but as pictures: 'tis the eye of childhood
That fears a painted devil. If he do bleed,
I'll gild the faces of the grooms withal,
For it must seem their guilt. (2.2.53–57)

But Macbeth is really worried. He asks,

> Will all great Neptune's Ocean wash
> this blood
> Clean from my hand? (2.2.60–61)

The next crisis to be faced is the discovery of the crime. At line 64, she realizes that their hands have the same colors, and at line 67 she says,

> A little water clears us of this deed.
> (2.2.67)

How easy and simple it appears to Lady Macbeth to cover the murder. She takes the bloodied weapon, making her own hands almost as bloody as Macbeth's. There is a pause here when perhaps the two of them have deep thoughts about the crucial nature of their actions. But quickly, she again takes the initiative, incriminating the grooms in the murder of Duncan.

Lennox and Macduff discover the murder and go into a panic. There is theatrical behavior from Macbeth and Lady Macbeth. When she enters at line 74, she asks what is happening, what is the reason for such a noise, and she plays her part, conveying the notion that she feels special responsibility for what happens in her house. Macduff and

Banquo do not talk to her directly, maybe because they think that this political crisis is not a matter for women to be involved in.

Duncan's sons enter at line 90, and Lady Macbeth plays her best role. She is on the point of collapse and asking for help. But the men continue talking of the horror of the

most bloody piece of work (2.3.123)

Everybody exits, and only Malcolm and Donalbain remain on stage. They are confused; perhaps they are speculating on whom the murderer could be. They are afraid; their minds must be volcanoes as they think about the murder, but they do not mention any names. Malcolm decides to go to England, and Donalbain decides to go to Ireland. They are the nearest allied in blood; one of them must be the next king, but they prefer to run away to save their lives. The brothers do not want to know even who has killed their father. They are afraid to know who committed

This murderous shaft that's shot (2.4.135)

From this precise moment, Macbeth is the king. The premonitions of the witches are fulfilled, and Lady Macbeth must be happy because her dreams have come true. Now she is the queen with all the power and all the glamour that this implies. The play is brought from intense excitement to a silenced reflection of what has happened and what is going to happen later on.

Banquo enters at the first line of act 3. His salutation to Macbeth is expected:

> Thou hast it now, King, Cawdor, Glamis, all,
> As the Weird Women promised
> (3.1.1–2)

Banquo and Macbeth have talked about the witches in previous scenes, but they do not this time. Maybe Macbeth wants Banquo to forget the other promises of the witches.

1.4 Lady Macbeth: The Queen

When Macbeth and Lady Macbeth enter in act 3, they are already crowned and robed, providing an image of kingship and enjoyment of the golden crown, which has been in their ambitious imaginations since some time before. The first lines of Lady Macbeth as the queen tell us about the kind of woman she is and the kind of queen she will be.

She says that King Duncan is forgotten already. We do not have to cry for him, she tells everyone. Let's have a great party and forget what has happened before. She feels complete now. She is the queen. She is enjoying the moment, and she wants everybody in the court to celebrate the happiness of her reign with her.

Meanwhile, Macbeth is afraid of Banquo because of the prophecies. He begins a plan to eliminate him. The witches have said that the descendants of Banquo, not those of Macbeth, will be kings. With this in mind, Macbeth talks with two murderers and convinces them that Banquo is their enemy. At the same time, he tells the murderers that Fleance, the son of Banquo, has no importance to him and that they can kill Fleance too. The murderers kill Banquo while he is outside the palace before the party is prepared. But Fleance, the son of Banquo, escapes.

At the beginning of scene 2, Lady Macbeth adopts different characters each time she talks. At the first line, she asks the servant:

Is Banquo gone from court? (3.2.1)

And later, she asks Macbeth,

What's to be done? (3.2.44)

In these two lines, Lady Macbeth appears to us like an innocent woman. She ignores everything that is happening in the palace, and she knows nothing about state matters. She knows that she and her husband need more crimes, more destruction, and more blood; they need the murder of Banquo. But she is again playing a role. She knows perfectly her husband's fears, but she is trying to forget the crime and tries to support him. In doing so, she says some interesting lines.

What's done is done. (3.2.12)

Here, Lady Macbeth reflects the personality of a very cold woman. It is no matter what they have done; to kill the king and give the order to kill their friend Banquo, saying that it is nothing to her, is remarkable. The coolness that Lady Macbeth shows in this line has made it one of the most famous lines of the play and, therefore, one of the most-used phrases of Shakespeare's worldwide.

Since Lady Macbeth knows that she is the queen, she also gives commands, as most queens are supposed to do. She enters in this scene with a servant, and she sends him to

> Say the King, I would attend his leisure
> For a few words (3.2.3)

Now that she is the queen, even her husband has to wait for her, and she has only seconds to talk with him. She realizes that she is in charge as the lady of the castle, and she immediately takes charge of the role.

At line 27 she changes again, and she becomes tender with her husband. Macbeth enters the scene describing his fears of being poisoned and of going mad. Lady Macbeth with words of motherhood says to him,

> Gentle my lord, sleek o'er your rugged looks;
> Be bright and jovial among your guests tonight (3.2.27–28)

Her husband is worried about their future, but she is only thinking about the party they will have in the palace. And Macbeth answers to her tenderness,

> So shall I, love, and so, I pray, be you
> (3.2.29)

He speaks affectionately. He uses the word *love*, as at the beginning of this act when he called her *dear wife* (3.2.36), or as when he called her *my dearest love* and *dearest chuck* (3.2.45). This means that love exists between them, in spite of the horror they are living.

This dialogue is of a very deep significance because we do not know if it is true that Lady Macbeth ignores the plans of her husband to kill Banquo. She sees that her husband is desperate, almost sick, thinking about what is done, and she consoles him, saying,

> You must leave this. (3.2.35)

But how can he leave something that is just beginning? And he answers her,

> O, full of scorpions is my mind dear wife!
> Thou know'st that Banquo and his Fleance lives (3.2.36–37)

Lady Macbeth tells him that as human beings, they are not immortal and that they will die sooner or later. Macbeth mentions the witches, but she tries to forget the witches, or at least she tries to give the appearance that she does not remember the prophecies. Then she poses an innocent question,

What's to be done? (3.2.45–46)

It seems here that she is excluded from her husband's plan to kill Banquo. His response is more tender than before, but he decides to tell her nothing. As a husband who wants to avoid a headache for his wife, he determines,

Be innocent of the knowledge, dearest chuck,
Till thou applaud the deed. (3.2.45–46)

That is, it is better for you and for your soul to ignore the details now, but later you will be happy with the results.

They have already entered the banquet, and Lady Macbeth asks her husband to give the welcome to their guests. Suddenly Macbeth sees one of the murderers and goes to speak with him. The murderer reports to Macbeth the details of Banquo's death and how Fleance ran away. While this is happening at a corner of the party room, Lady Macbeth is worried only about what is happening in the banquet. This is her first party as queen; she wants to be a good host. Then she calls the attention of her husband, telling him again with tenderness,

> My royal lord,
> You do not give the cheer. The feast is sold (3.4.32–34)

Russell points out that in the line "My royal lord," Lady Macbeth claims his attention as husband, as king, and as a master. They are having their first meeting with their friends as king and queen, and he is forgetting the basic rules of a court.

What happens later when Macbeth is sure that Banquo is sitting at his chair is simply pathetic. Lady Macbeth looks at and hears her husband with tension. Her mind is burning, but she is conscious that the success of this first royal party depends on her, and she will do whatever is necessary to have a wonderful party. Macbeth continues talking to the ghost of Banquo, and then Ross tries to help in the terrible situation, asking the guests to leave the room because the king is not feeling well. But Lady Macbeth insists that they stay. Then she questions her husband,

Are you a man? (3.4.57)

She is questioning his manhood again, but she is also terrified, first for her husband's apparent insanity and second because everybody heard when he was talking to the invisible ghost and mentioned the gory locks. Lady Macbeth is suffering a lot. All her dreams could disappear in a moment, so she complains to Macbeth,

> This is the very painting of your fear;
> This is the air-drawn dagger which you said (3.4.60–61)

He is still watching and speaking to the image of the ghost of Banquo. Lady Macbeth, in trying to solve the problem, this time asks him to be silent and to go to bed. He continues speaking, and he remembers that the witches also said,

> Blood will have blood (3.5.120)

He is tormented, almost crazy, but he tells Lady Macbeth that he will meet the Weird Sisters the next day because there are other things he needs to know.

This is the last time they are together in a scene. She is mentally well. She has remained in control during the horrible scene of the feast, and even with pity, she comforts her husband and draws him away to bed. There is a tense dialogue between them because Lady Macbeth cannot believe or understand what is happening with her husband. The plans were fulfilled without problems. They appear innocent to most of the people in the palace, and that must be a triumph. Then Macbeth mentions Macduff, and Lady Macbeth asks innocently,

Did you send to him, sir? (3.5.129)

This phrase is of a very special importance because we know already that Macbeth said before that he does not want his wife to be conscious of all the horrors he has in mind. But maybe Shakespeare also wanted to give us the impression that Lady Macbeth really is innocent of everything. Many critics agree that Lady Macbeth has nothing to do with the crimes incubated within and the guilty thoughts that torture Macbeth. R. A. Foakes points out,

She may be innocent of the deed, but she cannot escape the knowledge that corrodes her mind … Lady Macbeth suppresses her fears and, for a time, her knowledge, and is able to take in charge; but eventually her knowledge, her guilt, surfaces when she is unconscious, in the famous sleep-walking scene, in which she continually washes her hands, long after the Event, in a vain effort to cleanse herself of blood and murder.

The last lines between Macbeth and Lady Macbeth in the play are like a normal conversation of a married couple ready to sleep, talking about their domestic affairs. But in their case, the problems are serious because they are talking about murders. Macbeth says that his head is full of strange things, and the last words of Lady Macbeth to him are,

> You lack the season of all natures, sleep (3.5.140)

These words reveal exactly the mental condition of Macbeth. Now his life is full of desperate moments with lack of stability, dark visions, delirium, phantasms, ghosts, blood, madness, and craziness—some of the forces that will finish the reign of the Macbeths.

1.5 Lady Macbeth, a Tragic Woman

The witches promised the Macbeths success, power, riches, and peace for all their nights and days to come. But all this quickly turned into ashes, destroying not only their relationship but also the lives of many other people around them.

We move to the last act. At the beginning of scene 1, a doctor and a gentlewoman are talking about Lady Macbeth. Here we have the famous sleepwalking scene of Lady Macbeth. She walks asleep, with her eyes open, always with a light before her, rubbing her hands, talking about spots of blood on her hands and trying to make them disappear. This scene is also called the Mad Scene.

This part of the play concludes with repeated references to blood, blood that will never disappear—allusions to the murder of Duncan. She also remembers Lady Macduff and Banquo and makes references to time and to the bell knocking at the gate.

In this last act of Lady Macbeth, we find these famous and conclusive verses:

Here's the smell of the blood still:

> all the perfumes of Arabia will not sweeten
> this little hand. O, O, O! (5.1.40–41)

She clearly expresses panic. She does not want to sleep; she wants to escape from the terror of her dreams and nightmares. Illogical, irrational, and displeased desires along with new revelations of thoughts and feelings prepare us for the end of her part and her life in the story. Other aspects of her last intervention are the many references to Macbeth—his worries, his fears, his whiteness, and his unwillingness to go to bed.

> Wash your hands, put on your night-gown,
> Look not so pale: I tell you yet again, Banquo's buried;
> He cannot come out on's grave. (5.1.50–52)

We are not sure if she is really suffering of somnambulism or if she is already crazy. We do not know if she is conscious of what she said earlier:

> What's done is done. (5.1.55)

What is true is that now she is showing her own terror and her readiness to enter directly into hell. It is also true that she needs her husband. She leaves the scene obsessed by the need to be with her husband. The conclusion of her appearance in the play emphasizes the danger to her life and the danger to the kingdom.

The last time we hear of Lady Macbeth in the play is when Macbeth, entering scene 5, is giving commands to Seyton, an officer who attends him. They are preparing for war, and suddenly, they hear the cry of a woman. Macbeth asks Seyton what the noise is, and Seyton exits to investigate. Macbeth continues talking about his fears. A simple cry makes all the hair on his skin stand. Then, Seyton enters and tells Macbeth,

> The Queen, my lord, is dead. (5.5.16)

It seems that Macbeth was waiting for the death of Lady Macbeth because his reaction to her fatal end is,

> She should have died hereafter; …
> Life's but a walking shadow, a poor player.
> That struts and frets his hour upon the stage
> And then is heard no more. It is a tale

Told by an idiot, full of sound and fury,
Signifying nothing. (5.5.17–28)

Russell says that we can find biblical implications and allusions in these lines, in Psalm 22:15 and 39:7 and in Job 14:1–2 and 18:6. Perhaps Macbeth has repented and at this moment he is remembering his religious instructions. Maybe Macbeth is insensitive to his wife's death, or maybe he is so surprised, so astonished at her loss, that he is only trying to cover up the silent suffering and is unable to find the words to express his feelings (151).

Interestingly, in an experiment carried out by Marvin Rosenberg in which people who had never read the play read only the fifth scene of the first act, most of them assumed that it was Lady Macbeth who had committed the murder.

Lady Macbeth, like Desdemona in *Othello*, is not the same kind of person at the beginning of the play as she is at the end. The weakness of the woman comes out once again. Lady Macbeth is not able to handle her situation. She is not able to accept that she is responsible too, and she gives up in the face of that reality.

Macbeth is a play of sin, wrongdoing, delinquency, and tyranny; these are the many faces of a despotic oppressor. The good and the bad are always together; "men are neither good nor evil" (11). It is the atmosphere breathed by Shakespeare, an atmosphere charged with wars, crimes, and a dictatorship.

Most critics believe that Macbeth is the only tragic figure in the play, but we must remember that it is Lady Macbeth who suffers shame, penitence, regret, remorse, and frightening dreams. The problem is that Shakespeare entitled the play *Macbeth,* not *The Macbeths* or *Lady Macbeth*.

Chapter 3

Cleopatra in Shakespeare's *Antony and Cleopatra*

1.1 Literary Background of the Play

Behind *Antony and Cleopatra,* as with most of Shakespeare's plays, we find a source, perhaps more than one. Separated by fifteen centuries, Shakespeare found his inspiration in the work of the Greek biographer Plutarch, who gave him a very important literary contribution with his *Parallel Lives of Noble Greeks and Romans.* This historical document was translated into English by Sir Thomas North, who made the translation from the French version, which was translated by Jacques Amyot (1559). The first publication of North's was in 1579, but the publication of 1595 was the major source, not only of his *Antony and Cleopatra* but also of *Julius Caesar, Timon of Athens,* and *Coriolanus.* In the work of Plutarch, Shakespeare found detailed narrative biographies of his subjects, drawing parallels between Greeks and Romans, especially such outstanding figures as Julius Caesar and Alexander the Great. Plutarch and Shakespeare were interested in how people in power shape history and also in how people remember their lives.

Shakespeare tells us the same story as found in Plutarch's prose, but Shakespeare presents it in verse. One clear example is Enobarbus's description of Cleopatra's travel on her barge down the Cydnus River.

> [Cleopatra] disdained to set forward otherwise,
> but to take her barge in the River of Cydnus, the
> people whereof was of gold, the sailes of purple,
> and the owers of silver, which kept stroke in rowing
> after the sounde of the musicke of flutes, howboyes,
> citherns, viols, and such other instruments as they
> played upon a barge. (Gaines, 9)

This is the opening description in prose of North's translation of Plutarch. Now we have the same paragraph written in verse by Shakespeare:

The barge she sat in, like a burnished throne,
burned on the water. The poop was beaten
gold; purple the sails, and so perfumed that
the winds were lovesick with them: the oars
were silver, which to the tune of flutes kept
stroke, and made the water which they beat
to follow faster, as amorous of their strokes. (2.2.201–207)

Plutarch's *Antony* is his longest biography, and Shakespeare had to cut the narration to make it into a drama. However, Shakespeare's purpose with the story is the special, deep, and passionate relationship between the famous couple. He always allows them to recognize and to reveal the greatness of their love. "Life in its natural spontaneity is set against machination to satisfy a universal human need" (Colie, 63).

Many other famous writers had used the story written by Plutarch. Cinthio had also written his version of *Cleopatra*, which was acted in 1540 and published in 1583. Cinthio's story concentrates on Cleopatra. He promised that very few attentions would be on Antony, who appears only in three scenes, including where he encounters Cleopatra and where he is dying. Cinthio's play concerns Cleopatra's preparation for death, but at the end, the queen perishes of passion and of a broken heart.

Other writers and dramatists also wrote about Cleopatra. Jodelle presented a tragedy named *Cleopatra Captive* in 1552 and published it in 1574. The story is about the last day of its heroine's life. Antony appears only at the beginning as a Senecan ghost because he is recently dead. He is yearning for his lady's company in the underworld, wanting her to suffer the same infernal torture. The poor queen kills herself, maybe disappointed and sad.

In 1578, Garnier's tragedy *Antonie* appeared. It was translated into English by the Countess of Pembroke in 1590. Following Cinthio, the play opens at Actium, and the lovers are separated one from the other. In fact, we never see them together until the last scene, when Antonie is dead. Cleopatra, "an honest and tender-hearted woman, collapses over his corpse" (Barton, 42).

These dramatists pick up the story late in its development. They try to concentrate on Cleopatra at the expense of Antony, and they show us the lovers when they are together. All of them dignify Cleopatra herself, according to the requirements of the time and space they belong to.

Samuel Daniel's *Cleopatra* seems to be the most important from Shakespeare's point of view. It was conceived as a companion piece to the Countess of Pembroke's *Antonie* and published in 1599. There is no doubt that Shakespeare knew about and was greatly influenced by this play. Kenneth Muir identified a number of similarities between Shakespeare and Daniel, as well as differences and additions made by them to the story of Plutarch. It seems that it was Daniel's story that suggested to Shakespeare that Cleopatra was aging and worried about it and also that her death scene recreated the glory of Cydnus. Daniel's Cleopatra, in her first soliloquy, makes a confession that is unique to his play. She says that she has been loved by so many men in her life that "I to stay on love had never leisure."

1.2 Cleopatra: A Woman in History

We have and need to know a little of the events that occurred in and around the time and life of Cleopatra. It was one of the most turbulent and fascinating periods of history. Knowing these facts will help us to understand certain references and comments in the play.

Ptolemy Lagos was a general of Alexander the Great's. When his master died, Ptolemy appointed himself as governor of Egypt in the year 324 BC. A year later, Ptolemy became king of Egypt and founded a dynasty. Cleopatra was born in 69 BC in Alexandria, the capital of Egypt at that time. Her father was Egypt's pharaoh, Ptolemy XII, nicknamed Auletes or "Flute Player." Cleopatra's mother was probably Auletes's sister, Cleopatra V Tryphaena, because it was common for members of the Ptolomaic dynasty to marry their siblings to keep the empire, power, goods, and fortunes (18).

Cleopatra had an elder sister named Cleopatra VI. She also had an older sister named Berenice and a younger one called

Arsinoe. She also had two younger brothers called Ptolemy, and all her forefathers had this same name. Ptolemy is not an Egyptian name but a Macedonian name—originally Ptolemaus. Cleopatra's father was a weak and cruel ruler. In 58 BC, the people of Alexandria rebelled against him. He escaped to Rome, and his daughter Berenice took the throne. She married a cousin but later strangled him. At this time, Cleopatra VI died of an unknown disease. Then Ptolemy XII reclaimed his throne with the help of Pompey, the Roman general. He beheaded his daughter Berenice and her new husband too.

Cleopatra was probably eleven years old when she became the queen of Egypt. She had an enchanting musical voice, as reported by Plutarch from many sources contemporary with Cleopatra. She spoke more than seven languages, including Greek, Latin, Persian, Aramaic, and ancient Egyptian. She was the first Ptolemy pharaoh who learned the language of her people, and with this she proved to be a great politician.

According to Egyptian tradition, Cleopatra married her brother Ptolemy XIII, who was about twelve years old. It was a marriage of convenience, and Ptolemy was pharaoh in name only. A eunuch named Pothinus advised Ptolemy to conspire against Cleopatra. They took power, and Cleopatra was forced into exile in Syria.

Cleopatra formed an army on Egypt's border, determined to get back to her throne. Meanwhile, Pompey sailed to Alexandria to seek Ptolemy's protection after having lost the battle at Pharsalos. When Pompey arrived, Ptolemy's advisors killed him and gave his head as a gift to Caesar. Caesar disliked the brutal murder of his former friend. Caesar entered Alexandria, took control of the city and the palace, and asked for the presence of Ptolemy and Cleopatra. But she was afraid of her brother Ptolemy, so she had herself brought to Caesar inside an Oriental rug. It is said that Caesar was bewitched by her charm and became her lover that very night.

After this, the Egyptians and the Romans had a war for six months. Finally, Caesar restored Cleopatra to her throne. History has said that the love couple enjoyed a leisurely two-month cruise on the Nile River. Cleopatra may have become pregnant at this time with her son Ptolemy XV, called Caesarion or "Little Caesar." After the cruise, Caesar returned to Rome and asked Cleopatra to live in a villa near there. However, the Romans did not approve of Caesar's actions. They thought that Cleopatra was a danger to Rome and that Caesar intended to become king of Rome, and it was also rumored that he wanted to marry Cleopatra and make their son his heir. For all these suppositions, he was killed by Brutus in front of the senate. Cleopatra knew that she was in danger, too, so she left Rome quickly with her son and went to Egypt.

Caesar's murder brought chaos, anarchy, and civil disorder to Rome. The empire was divided into three parts: one part for Caesar's great-nephew Octavian, who later became the Emperor Augustus; a second part to Marcus Lepidus; and the third one for Marcus Antonius—Mark Antony to us.

Cleopatra met Antony in the year 41 BC at Tarsus (Turkey today) because he wanted to ask her if she had assisted his enemies. Boltin Lee says that Cleopatra arrived in style on a

> barge with gilded stern, purple sails, and silver oars. The boat was sailed by her maids, who were dressed as

sea nymphs. Cleopatra was dressed as Venus, the goddess of love. She was reclined under a golden canopy, fanned by boys in Cupid costumes.

Antony, an ingenuous, naïve, and joy-loving man, was intimidated by her display of luxury, and it is precisely here that Shakespeare's play begins.

1.3 Cleopatra: A Woman and a Queen in Love

When we read about and try to analyze the Cleopatra of Shakespeare's play, many questions come to mind. At the end, many of our questions about her remain unanswered. But we cannot separate the woman from the queen because they are together throughout the play. We really do not know if she is a good person or a bad person, if she is important or unimportant. Another critic suggests that Cleopatra represents Egypt and Antony represents Rome. If this is so, and the "crucial dialectic is between Egypt and Rome, the play does not resolve, does not progress, does not reach any kind of tragic climax" (Bamber, 111).

Within the play, Enobarbus has his own

interpretation about Cleopatra. He says that she must be understood in terms of

> Her infinity variety. Other woman cloy (2.2.245)

According to him, she is a woman who is difficult to predict, a woman whose moods are changeable and whose personality is many-sided. She is more than one kind of character; that is why she provokes so many disagreements among critics. Linda Bamber believes that there are three different Cleopatras in the play.

> At one level she is the embodiment of Egypt and a symbol of our antihistorical experience. At another level she represents the Other as against Antony's representation of the Self. And finally Cleopatra is a character like Antony himself, facing failure and defeat motivated by the desire to contain or rise above her losses. (109)

Cleopatra is many things, especially for Antony. She means for him satisfaction, enjoyment, power, and fecundity, but also a kind of corrosion. Cold Rome has nothing to do with the heat and tenderness of her body.

She represents Egypt to Antony. When he returns to Rome, he tells Lepidus,

> The higher Nilus swells
> The more it promises; as it ebbs, the seedsman
> Upon the slime and ooze scatters his grain,
> And shortly comes to harvest (2.7.20–23)

We must remember that Egypt was the grain store of the Roman Empire. A third of the corn feeding Italy came from Egypt; therefore, Egypt was vital to Rome. The language used in the play sometimes gives us enough action and judgment, but not the meaning. We get the meaning in the characters' attitudes toward the language they are using. Rome is contractual obligation, a sense of duty, political affairs, and honor. Rome is also another kind of public life. Egypt is gentleness, luxury, sensuality, and entertainment. Egypt is "the East" where the beds are soft. But we do not have in the play the meaning of that "bed" (Colie, 57).

There is a little difference between Cleopatra as Egypt and Cleopatra as the Other. It is that, as Egypt, she represents the Other;

Egypt and Rome represent the opposite options to the hero Antony, a reality external to the Self with which the hero is confronted in tragedy. The discussion between the Self and the Other reflects the relation of the hero with women, which apparently is always resolved in tragedy.

Antony returns to Egypt after a drunken party on a boat. After Egypt, the corruption of Rome comes out, the old world is gone, and Antony decides to live in the new world, the world of the Other, an opposite to Rome. Cleopatra clearly identifies with Egypt, and Antony's relationships with Cleopatra are phases in his response to the new world (111).

The third Cleopatra, according to Bamber, is the one who vigorously resists Antony's travel to Rome. She is angry and jealous, she does not want to hear his reasons, and she is

Quickly ill, and well (1.3.71)

It is a strong and deep feeling. There are some lines of intimate conversation.

Let us go. Come;
Our separation so abides and flies

> That thou, residing here, goes yet
> with me,
> And I, hence fleeting, here remain
> with thee.
> Away! (1.3.102–105)

These lines give us the only moment in an emotional and intense scene where the audience can understand how much the two love each other. Cleopatra seems vulnerable as in no other scene before. Their hearts are beating hard while leaving, and to Cleopatra, it is a high price to pay as a person and also as a ruler of a great empire.

Cleopatra seems to substitute herself for her feelings. She does not pretend to feel something she is not feeling. But her feelings do not threaten her consciousness of being herself, "as broad as she has breadth, at all times and places," says Bamber. "Under similar circumstances of loss, the tragic Self, by contrast, invariably suffers a loss of identity more painful than the material loss itself."

Antony and Cleopatra is a play about war, politics, and most of all, love. When Cleopatra enters in act 1, scene 1, she begins asking

Antony how much and how far he loves her.
Antony answers,

> Then must thou needs find out new
> heaven,
> new earth. (1.1.18)

This line sets the story and establishes the magnitude of his love for her. He is clear in how much he loves her, but she does not mention—and of course we ignore—the measure of her love for him.

They are talking pleasantly, and a messenger interrupts their conversation with news from Rome. Cleopatra immediately reacts as a jealous woman. She is angry because she assumes that Fulvia, his wife in Rome, wants Antony's presence. She also thinks that it could be Caesar who sends orders to Antony. But he answers with sweet words, like those from a poem of love.

> Let Rome in Tiber melt and the wide
> arch
> of the ranged empire fall; here is my
> space.
> Kingdoms are clay; our dungy earth
> alike (1.1.35–37)

But she answers that his words are falsehood, that she is not a fool to believe that he married Fulvia without loving her. She is acting simply as a jealous woman. He does not pay attention to her defiance. He embraces her to his heart, seduces her to forget the messenger and the news, and invites her to enjoy every minute they are living in pleasure.

After this brief dialogue between the lovers, Cleopatra does not appear again until some time later. Other characters enter the scene talking about different topics, where we can learn about their vanity, their religious beliefs, geography, and so on. In part, we learn about the death of Fulvia in Sycion. Antony feels truly sorry about her death, and Enobarbus, his loyal friend and soldier, tells him,

> Why, then we kill all our women. We see how
> mortal an unkindness is to them. If they suffer
> our departure, death's the word.
> (1.1.27–29)

Antony knows that Fulvia's death has too much to do with Cleopatra. Enobarbus consoles

Antony by reminding him of Cleopatra's kindness. Janet Suzman thinks that from line 131 to 137, Enobarbus is talking about orgasm, lovemaking, anxiety over dying, and enjoying sex. He defends Cleopatra, describing her force and her energy when she is in command of any enterprise. Suzman also thinks that Enobarbus could be half in love with Cleopatra and that maybe he is jealous of Antony (19).

Cleopatra enters at the beginning of scene 3, asking for Antony.

> See where is he, who's with him, what
> he does.
> I did not send you. If you find him sad,
> Say I am dancing; if in mirth, report
> that I am sudden sick. Quick, and
> return. (1.3.1–5)

As Suzman says, "She sets the full Alexandrian spying-machine in motion" (23).

And here, of course, she is acting both as a woman and as a queen. The jealous woman is worried about what her man is doing. But as a queen, she must be careful because Antony's military machine could know that she is spying on him. That is why she tells Charmian to deny that she sent her. Charmian gives her some advice.

> In each thing give him away, cross him in nothing (1.3.9)

But stubbornness is prevalent in Cleopatra, and she tells Charmian, "That is to act as a fool," that it is an easy way to lose Antony, and that she is precisely fighting to keep him and his love with her.

In the first appearance of Cleopatra and Antony in the play, they talk about their love all the time. They are enchanted with each other. But their problems begin because of Cleopatra's constant fights with her inner self. The play does not give us continuous details of her point of view; we are not close to her for more than a few speeches. However, in those few moments, we can speculate on her real motives and goals.

Antony enters in line 14, and Cleopatra simulates—or maybe she is really near to suffer—a collapse. He, as always, talks to her with sweet words.

> Now my dearest queen (1.3.18)
> Most sweet queen (1.3.32)
> How now, my lady? (1.3.39)

My precious queen, forbear (1.3.75)

She begins to talk without stopping a minute, and he has a chance to say only a few words in between. She is really a woman and a queen upset.

> I have no power upon you; hers you
> are. (1.3.23)
> Why should I think you can be mine,
> and true (1.3.28)

She is desperate; she believes that her love is going to the arms of his legitimate wife. She shows her fears of the inexorable travel of Antony to Rome with an emotional speech of jealousy.

> Eternity was in our lips and eyes
> (1.3.35)

She doubts. If their affair has been a lie for Antony, if his promises of love were false, she is guilty of believing them. Finally, Antony can talk, and he tells her that the real reason for his departure is that his wife has died. He talks straight to her, and this is an important element in their relationship because they are bound by a mutual passion.

Cleopatra's reaction is unpredictable. She

talks about age. Since she is worried about age, she thinks that Fulvia is too young to die. In these crucial moments, Cleopatra oscillates to words of disbelief. She tells Antony,

> O, most false love!
> Where be the sacred vials thou shouldst fill
> with sorrowful water? Now I see, I see,
> In Fulvia's death, how mine received shall be. (1.3.62–65)

She is a woman talking, manipulating the situation, trying to convince herself that she is right, that she has the only truth. Now she knows what his reaction will be when she dies. She looks selfish in these lines:

> Then bid adieu to me, and say the tears Belong to Egypt. (1.3.77–78)

She is probably crying here, as most women do in a situation like this. She is reminding him of what they have lived together, how they have loved each other. But she is also asking him to forget everything. To stop her attempts to retain him, he must leave. There is a lonely silence after the separation. Linda Fitz believes that we must understand

Cleopatra from inside since "Shakespeare takes pains to let Cleopatra explain her contrary behavior and give the reason for it. She struggles with her own inconstancy and learns and grows as Antony does not."

It is a long time before we see them together again. But we must keep in mind this part of the story because, here, Cleopatra is acting clearly as a woman in love but also as a queen. As a queen, she wants to force Antony to stay with her with the force of their love and the force she has as the queen of Egypt.

In the play, the setting moves from Egypt to Rome. Lepidus and Caesar talk about the victories of Pompey at sea, and they need an alliance with Antony. War is only for men. That is the way Romans think.

After this scene 4 in Rome, we come back to Cleopatra's palace. We see Cleopatra again in scene 5. Now she is impulsive, giving commands, maybe shouting, calling her attendants, as a queen, with imperative orders. She is angry.

There is an interesting dialogue here between the queen and the eunuch Mardian.

She is asking him if he has affections. The question's meaning is whether he has a sexual appetite. The eunuch answers,

> Yes gracious madam. ... I can do nothing,
> Yet I have fierce affections, and think what Venus did to Mars (1.5.10–18)

It seems to us that Cleopatra is all the time thinking about sex. She forgets that she is a queen here and acts as an ordinary woman. In the following lines, we find again words that appear to be about sex.

> Is he on his horse?
> O happy horse, to bear the weight of Antony! ...
> Where's my serpent of old Nile? (1.5.22–26)

Cleopatra's imagination is working. Sex is a reality for her, and the imagination is full of a fantasy of love and sensuality. The two fuse in these lines referring to Antony's absence. Colie says, "Her images of weight are realistic and are enough in any woman's experience of love. She attributes to her demi-Atlas more weight than any man can carry."

Now she has the first report about Antony since he left. We must remember here that a journey in those days could be of great danger and took a long time because of the distances traveled and because of the different wars in the region.

At the end of this scene, she also says, "My man of men" (1.5.73). We can compare this line with Desdemona's—"My dear Othello" (2.1.78)—and with Lady Macbeth's—"My royal lord" (4.4.32).

To Desdemona, a young girl in love, the words have the simplicity of their meaning. To Lady Macbeth, the words have respect for her royal husband. For Cleopatra, the phrase means also possession. Antony is her possession, as she is Antony's possession. "Man of men" refers to the fact that, as she has said before, she has had many men, but Antony is her real love. There is no comparison with the men she had before. To her, the earth is smaller than this man.

Act 2 is a very long act in which many things occur. Pompey says that it is impossible for Antony to leave Cleopatra to fight together with Lepidus and Caesar against him. The legendary sexuality of Cleopatra incites envy in young males.

In another scene, Caesar welcomes Antony to Rome, reminding him that he is the owner of the third part of the world,

> But not such a wife. (2.2.52)

Romans do not like Cleopatra; she is a danger for the Roman Empire. Caesar, Antony, and Lepidus are talking of state matters in front of Agrippa and Enobarbus. And it is Agrippa who suggests that Antony marry Octavia.

> To hold you in perpetual amity,
> To make you brothers, and to knit your
> hearts (2.2.133–134)

Antony accepts.

> Let me have thy hand.
> Further this act of grace, and from this hour
> The heart of brothers governs in our loves. (2.2.155–157)

From these lines, we know why Antony marries Octavia. Antony also tells her,

> Shall all be done by the rule. (2.3.7)

And she will accept, too, because her loving brother says, "Do it," for his sake and for Rome's, and most of all to keep Cleopatra out of Rome. That is one of the reasons this is a play about politics and also about foreign affairs.

However, after the marriage, Antony says,

> I will go to Egypt;
> And though I make this marriage for my peace,
> I' the East my pleasure lies. (2.5.38–40)

He will go to Cleopatra. He has nothing to do in Rome with Octavia. In marrying Octavia, he knows what exactly Cleopatra means to him.

Cleopatra reappears in scene 5. As always, she enters giving orders, as a queen. In a disconcerted action, she invites the eunuch to play with her:

> Let's to billiards. (2.5.3)

According to Suzman, this line has a sexual connotation because billiards refer to balls, and Cleopatra, as a liberated woman, can talk with her servants about sex. The woman, as well as the queen, wants to be busy.

Her memories go easily from happiness to sadness, from love memories to crude jealousy.

A messenger arrives from Rome, and Cleopatra, her mind with combustion and flames, thinks the worst. She believes that Antony is dead. She wants to know the message, but she is so nervous, as a woman could be in such cases. She offers the messenger gold if he says that Antony is alive but death if he says that Antony is dead. At last, the messenger tells her that Antony is well. The moment is full of tension. She talks incessantly, and the messenger has to tell her,

Will't please you hear me? (2.5.43)

After some lines, like in a word game, the man tells her that Antony has married Octavia. She does not want to hear it, does not want to believe what the servant is saying. She becomes angry, upset, and jealous. The woman and the queen are again in action. She offers to the messenger a province, half of Egypt, if he could tell her only what her heart and her senses want to hear. And the Egyptian investigator will have to work again.

Report the feature of Octavia, her
years,
her inclination. Let him not leave out.
The color of her hair. Bring no word
quickly. (2.6.13–15)

She is a queen acting as a woman or perhaps
a woman acting as a queen. Her sharp
curiosity is used by Shakespeare, combining
the comic and the tragic in this scene. In
the first three scenes of this act, Cleopatra
struggles to keep Antony with her, to avoid
his leaving her, but in scene 4, he is already
gone. And finally, in this scene, he has just
married Octavia.

In this scene in which Cleopatra learns that
Antony has married Octavia, Cleopatra is
his victim. But we must not take her side;
we must be careful about sympathizing
with her. Bamber says, "She is presented
here as unreasonable, willful, capricious and
jealous—not as wronged, hurt or sad."

In the following scenes, we have the meeting
of the three owners of the known world, in
which they talk with followers and servants.
They talk about war and possessions. Later,
they have a party on a boat, and as ordinary
men they talk about different themes, discuss

war results, accuse their enemies, excuse themselves, and drink and eat together, but they do not kill and do not fight anybody. And, we can add, some of them talk about Cleopatra, good or bad; she is always in the eye of the storm.

Caesar, Lepidus, and Antony are talking with Octavia. Caesar tells Antony,

> You take from me a great part of myself. (3.2.24)

He means, *Be careful, Antony. She is my dear sister, my child, and probably also my girl.* Some critics believe that there is an incestuous link between Octavia and Caesar. They are two hearts in real pain because of their imminent separation. Antony tells Caesar that he must not worry about her, that she will be all right.

> The April's in her eyes. It is love's spring. (3.2.43)

Antony is sure that Octavia's tears mean the beginning of her love for him. Octavia loves Antony already, and this is the opening of the future tragedies for them all.

Cleopatra says that she has nothing to do

when Antony is not with her. And once again, she asks a messenger about her rival's charms.

> Is she as tall as me? (3.3.13)
> Is she shrill-tongued or low? (3.3.15)
> Guess at her years, I prithee. (3.3.30)
> Bear'st thou her face in mind? Is't long or round? (3.3.33)

The man is a key witness for her. As a result of her natural woman's curiosity, she already has a verdict: Octavia is not tall and is low voiced. Cleopatra is sure that Antony dislikes that voice because Octavia is "dull tongued, and dwarfish." Octavia is a thirty-year widow with a round face and brown hair. Now, Cleopatra has a clear image of Octavia and feels that she has many advantages. Her rival is almost nothing; she is a superficial woman. She hears only what she wants to hear. She does not want to judge lie from truth, and of course there will be "gold" for the messenger—a man who tells her that Octavia is eight years older than she, an adversary not in her first flower because Octavia is a widow.

Antony is in Athens with Octavia. They live there two years. He is trying to convince her that he must go to battle against Pompey. Octavia comes back to Rome to tell her brother, but Caesar knows immediately that Antony is lying; he must be in Egypt with Cleopatra, to whom he has given his empire. Caesar is angry because Antony has disappointed him. He has broken their pact. Octavia must be suffering and frustrated, which is reason enough for Caesar, who loves his sister dearly, to begin a war.

Everybody in Rome thinks the same way, Antony's heart and brain are in Egypt, and nobody commands the war because Cleopatra, being a woman, is out of the war too.

> Sink Rome, and their tongues rot.
> I will not stay behind (3.7.15–16)

These lines come back to us from the queen, the pharaoh, the commander in chief, and the strong woman. Antony enters with Canidius talking about war. Cleopatra intervenes, but it seems that he does not hear her. He is determined to fight at sea, but if they fail, then they will fight on land. Cleopatra is afraid, but she has the most powerful fleet in the world. It is the first time they are together again in Egypt, but Antony is worried about what is happening outside.

The lovers meet again after line 25. But the mood, their feelings, and their thoughts are different. Antony has lost kingdoms and provinces in the battle. He comes back to the palace and is said to be "unqualitied with very shame" (3.11.44).

Eros and Iras want Cleopatra to console Antony. They announce her presence, but Antony is so depressed that he cannot look into her eyes. He has lost her sails and her people in the battle. Cleopatra says only,

Pardon, Pardon! (3.11.68)

She shows that she is his true conqueror. Antony is repelled by many people because of her. He is not respected by others because of his passing all the time with Cleopatra in Egypt and not taking care of his third of the world.

Suddenly, he asks her for a kiss. A kiss from his love is the only thing that can repair his desperate warrior heart. Suzman says that this kiss "is an infinitely tender full-hearted thing; they have never been closer and never more apart" (139). With her kisses and wine, his life is not over yet.

Caesar sends a courageous message to Cleopatra, saying that she must leave Antony. The ruler of the whole world wants her to abandon Antony, and she must be under his protection. She apparently accedes to the requirements of Caesar but only because she knows that it is the only way to survive. Antony is jealous and sends his servants to punish Caesar's messenger, Thidias. They scourge Thidias, and Antony recovers his personality little by little. He feels that he is in command again. Cleopatra is trying to get his attention, but he continues sending messages to Caesar. All of a sudden, he realizes that she is there, and he complains that she is sad and disconsolate. She responds with an overgenerous and excessive solution. She feels disgraceful and miserable, but Antony needs her. Then she swears the impossible, telling him exactly what he needs to hear—that she and the Egyptians will fight with him up to the end. He only answers,

I am satisfied. (3.13.169)

To his next speech, Cleopatra responds,

That's my brave lord! (3.13.179)

Because he is again talking like a general, Cleopatra makes a sweet and simple announcement: today is her birthday. Now they have a double cause to celebrate. We do not know if it is her real birthday or if she means that, now that Antony is himself again and her soul is at peace, she is reborn with happiness.

In act 4, the war has just begun. Caesar, knowing that Antony calls him "the boy," answers that Antony is a "ruffian," and from now they will have a personal combat. At Cleopatra's palace, Antony needs only two hours to rest before going to war. He has asked his "hearty friends" to weep. Cleopatra does not understand his words. She is separated, in silence. Her thoughts

lie too deep for tears, she is feeling searing pity. (161)

When the time comes to wake up, Antony calls Eros to put the armor on him. And "the most tender, playful, loving of all scenes" is in this dialogue. Cleopatra says to Antony, softly and with tenderness,

Sleep a little. (4.4.2)

Nay, I'll help too. (4.4.5)
Is not this buckled well? (4.4.11)

She wants to help, to be useful, to respond to these sweet words.

No, my chuck. (4.4.3)
The armorer of my heart. (4.4.8)

Antony wins this battle, and he needs Cleopatra to witness his triumph. He calls her my "nightingale" after she calls him "Lord of Lords." A party for everybody must be the best Roman and Egyptian way to share the victory. The next and final battle will be at sea. They know that Caesar will be better. Antony loses the battle, and his reaction targets Cleopatra. He calls her for the first time in the play "Egyptian," gypsy, and witch. He is violent, and this is the only moment in the play in which they are entirely alone. She runs away terrified and conceives a terrible and fatal lie—that she has killed herself. We think that here Cleopatra acts as some women do, who believe that by committing suicide, or only giving the appearance that they intend to do it, they will have their lovers' pity or repentance.

Antony assumes that she is really dead, so

he wants to die too, like a Roman soldier, with his own sword. Likely, he does not have the courage to do it himself, and he asks Eros to kill him. But in response, Eros kills himself as he is unable to kill his master. Antony says that Cleopatra and Eros are more valiant than he is, and then he falls on his own sword. He is mortally wounded when Diomedes comes with a message from Cleopatra. The messenger tells Antony that Cleopatra is alive, that she is locked in her monument, and the reasons she had in doing so.

Scene 15 of act 4 takes place inside the monument. Antony is almost dead, and Cleopatra is probably crying, desperate, kissing him, and trying to give him life. This is their last scene together, alive, and they talk like what they are—lovers. Antony says, calling her "Egypt" up to the end,

> Of many thousands kisses the poor last
> I lay upon thy lips. (4.5.21–22)

Cleopatra, with a sense of irony and sensuality, tells him,

> How heavy weighs my lord! (4.15.34)

He is dying, but she is still talking like a sensual woman. Her speech after Antony's death reveals to us that she is terrified. She is not the powerful queen anymore; she is, according to herself,

> No more but e'en a woman, and commanded
> By such poor passion as the maid that milks (4.15.77–78)

In front of her gods, she is only a woman, in spite of being the daughter of Isis. But her sufferings in these moments are greater than her faith. She challenges her gods. We can see here again that the woman and the queen are constantly together.

1.4 Cleopatra, a Tragic Woman

The last act of the play reminds us that this is a play of death too. Antony is already dead, and when Caesar learns of it, his reaction is filled with emotional words. His rivalry with Antony has given his short life purpose and shape, but he remembers Antony with words such as *companion, friend, mate, brother*, and so on, as a kind of reconciliation for what Antony represented for Rome and the Romans.

Cleopatra enters in scene 2. She is thinking that only suicide and death will give her a better life—the eternal life that she, as a goddess, will have, and most of all, because she will be with Antony again in their next and future life. She feels terrible, and now she holds the whole play on her shoulders. She is the queen of the great Egypt and other countries. She is conscious of what she represents for her people. A great fight must be in her head in that moment; the woman, the queen, and the mother are only one.

When Proculeius arrives with the message from Caesar, she remembers that Antony had told her that this is the only man of Caesar's she could trust. However, she is tough and arrogant with him. Intelligent as she is, she guesses that Antony was wrong and decides that she will not trust this man.

Cleopatra is determined in her purposes and goals. The only thing she wants is to conquer Egypt for her son, and she will be pleased if Caesar goes along with the idea because her son is a Ptolemy and must reign in Egypt. She also sends a message to Caesar that now she has learned a "doctrine of obedience" (5.2.31).

We know that it is not true. For the second time in the play, she is sending false messages to Caesar in order to gain time and his confidence. The first time was with the messenger Thidias.

Even in this crucial end of her life, after all the grief, sadness, pain, and sorrow for Antony's death, she is thinking only of Egypt and its people. She cannot give the Egyptians the spectacle of seeing their beloved queen being humiliated by Caesar and the Romans. But she is also thinking as a woman, who is also a mother and a queen. She is worried about who is going to inherit the throne of Egypt, her kingdom, and she wants it only for her son, Ptolemy Caesar. This is her priority throughout the play. That is the reason she ran to the arms of the great general Mark Antony right after the death of Julius Caesar. She wants to be safe and keep her son safe too. She also wants to rule Egypt, but Egypt had been conquered by the Romans many years ago. The Egyptians had to pay taxes to Rome, and the only way to survive as a queen was to form an alliance with Antony. But the queen, as a woman, succumbed to Antony's charms and fell in love with him. That is her real tragedy because Antony married Octavia, the dear sister of Caesar—her worst enemy in Rome—and the owner of the other part of the world. She is really afraid of what is going to happen to her at the hands of Caesar. She tries to kill herself with a dagger in front of Proculeius, who disarms her and begs her to wait to see the nobleness of Caesar. Now, Cleopatra makes a threat—she will not eat, drink, or sleep, and Caesar can do nothing to prevent it.

> Rather a ditch in Egypt
> Be gentle grave unto me! Rather on Nilus' mud
> Lay me stark naked and let the waterflies
> Blow me into abhorring! Rather make
> My country's high pyramids my gibbet
> And hang me up in chains!

The woman and the queen together again, she is thinking of many honorable ways to die, but in her homeland, near her people and her gods.

Dolabella and Proculeius, Iras, and others are always gentle with Cleopatra. They speak respectfully to her up to the end, according to what she is and deserves: majesty, queen, and sovereign, gentle madam, good madam, dear lady, royal queen, and so on.

At this point, Cleopatra knows that she needs an ally. She realizes already that Proculeius is not of her part, as Antony said before dying. Cleopatra tells Dolabella of a dream she had in which Antony was an emperor. But that was only a dream that cannot correspond to the moment in which they are living.

Caesar enters anxious and worried with a question that tells us the way he feels.

Which is the Queen of Egypt? (5.2.112)

He knows that he has conquered a great country and a great queen. He begs her not to arise in his presence. She is Egypt to the Romans, from the beginning to the end of the play. Cleopatra speaks to her masters with obedience. Caesar is also gentle with her, trying to convince her to stay alive. He advises her not to have bad thoughts. Caesar knows what she is thinking and tells her also,

Feed and sleep. (5.2.187)

A clear metaphor of what is happening is the meaning of the next lines from Iras.

Finish good lady. The bright day is done,
And we are for the dark. (5.2.193–194)

"The bright day" means all the years of splendor, luxury, wealth, and prosperity they have lived with Cleopatra as their queen. But now, they are ready for dark—a temporary dark only because later they will have eternity. According to the Egyptian traditions and beliefs, the queen and her servants will be together in the next life.

From line 207 to 220, Cleopatra sees terrible images of what is waiting for her in the streets of Rome.

> In gory detail the ghastly triumph through the
> streets of Rome; fetid breath, smelly armpits,
> grabbing hands, drunken songs, mocking pageants,
> and with a posture of a whore.

The vivid view of their future as Caesar's trophies of war serves to reinforce her courage and to help young Iras understand why she must take her own life. Iras is like a daughter to the queen. Throughout the play, we know that she had only one son, Ptolemy Caesar. However, Dolabella and Caesar talk about children.

Now, Cleopatra is ready to die, ready to assume the role of her greatness. She wants to be transformed into the goddess queen. She is the daughter of Isis, she is Egypt, and she is immortal. She wants to be dressed in the same way she was dressed when she met Antony on the river of Cydnus. In that way, she is ready to meet her lover, who is waiting for her. She is now like a bride preparing for her eternal wedding.

A rural fellow brings a basket with figs, but we know that it is only to avoid the curiosity of the guards. It is part of the plan because inside the basket is

> the pretty worm of Nilus, that kills and pains not, whose biting is immortal (5.2.243–244)

Cleopatra wants to know more about the "worm." Suddenly she asks,

> Will it eat me? (5.2.268)

We think that Shakespeare wants to give us a touch of innocence in the legendary queen. She asks this like an innocent child would ask. Perhaps she is not the woman that Plutarch and the Romans want us to believe she is. Maybe, because of a little phrase like this one, so many writers and film productions have dignified her character so we can make the decision to judge her in many different ways.

In her last speech, Cleopatra says that Antony is calling her. This is enough reason for her to die quickly. She takes the little snake to her breast, like a baby, as she says. Her last words before dying are about what she feels after the bite.

> As sweet as balm, as soft as air, as gentle—
> O Antony, Nay, I will take thee too.
> (5.2.305–306)

She compares her feelings in this moment with her love with Antony. Perhaps the comparison is because the kisses of Antony were also mortal to her. She is a woman, suffering as any mortal woman, up to her last breath.

Let's take a look at North's English translation of Plutarch's prose about Cleopatra's death:

> They founde Cleopatra starke dead,
> layed upon a bed of gold,
> attired and arrayed in her royal robes,

and one of her two women, which was
called Iras,
dead at her feete: and her other
woman called
Charmian halfe-dead, and trembling,
trimming the diademe which Cleopatra
ware upon her head.

Cleopatra won her last war against Caesar.
She died in the only way an Egyptian queen
should—enthroned, with her crown, inside
her monument, with her servants around
her, and showing again all the splendor
of her life and her reign. Everything was
programmed following the Egyptian tradition
to go together to live in the other life.

Caesar also gives his final opinion about
Cleopatra.

Bravest at the last,
she leveled at our purposes and, being
royal, took her own way. (5.2.331–333)

Some lines later, he also says,

O noble weakness!
If they can swallow poison, 't would
appear
By external swelling; but she looks
like sleep,

As she would catch another Antony
In her strong toil of grace. (5.2.341–344)

Even Caesar recognizes her beauty and says that now she is ready to conquer another man like Antony in her next life. Cleopatra dies perfectly as a tragic queen. Before dying, she emancipates the nature of Antony's death and also the reasons of her appearance at Cydnus, enthroned in gold, as the Goddess Isis. Cleopatra keeps her word to follow Antony after death. This fact has no parallel in other tragedies of Shakespeare; we *want* Cleopatra to die. It is the face of a normal hero. In *Othello*, we expect the possibility that Othello will get to the truth about Iago and recognize Desdemona's innocence before it is too late. Only in *Antony and Cleopatra* are we with the protagonist, who, unlike Macbeth, has not been a villain, to decide to die, and so she did. It alters the way we think about Cleopatra when we read the play for the first time. And it also makes it impossible for all writers of the story to criticize or condemn her, no matter the moral pattern of the work in which she appeared.

Conclusion

To talk about tragedies, we must go to ancient Greece, where the first tragedies were performed in honor of the God of Wine, Dionysius. Most of them were satiric or burlesque representations with men dancing and repeating songs, but later they became illustrations of the known relationship between men and gods. The representations were explanations to the audience that individuals make mistakes, that certain results could occur for those who behave in the same way, and the meaning of being a human and not a god or demigod.

For centuries, different schools and scholars have been dedicated to the study and meaning of literary criticism or literary analysis. But during the eighteenth century, an English essayist and literary historian, Samuel Johnson (1709–1784), began to investigate and write about this subject, at the same time analyzing many authors, including Shakespeare, with his only purpose being to help other people understand what they can while reading literature. He said that if we have problems understanding or interpreting Shakespeare, it's because he used proverbs, phrases, and words that were common to the way people spoke at that time. Johnson's analysis of Shakespeare is also intended to help us understand literature as a whole, and he argues that drama must be like life itself.

This is not the only theory we can find from the twentieth century. The 1920s brought the structuralism theory, the 1930s saw formalism and psychoanalytic criticism, and this was followed by feminist criticism in the 1960s and new historicism in the 1980s. We have many points of view about how to analyze and make criticisms about any book or poem and literature in general.

My work followed the reader-response criticism format. It was developed in America and Germany during the 1960s and has to do with the idea that it is not necessary to have a specific objective to read a book, a play, or any written masterpiece. Each reader gives his own interpretation and response according to his cultural, religious, historical, or political background.

Shakespeare is the writer of plays categorized as histories, comedies, and tragedies. In his tragedies, we can find many kinds of characters. Most of these plays have been studied as great psychological pieces of world literature. Their characters are ones whose behavior can be easily identified as representative of human beings throughout the times for their dramatic impact to achieve the development of the play. That is the case of the female characters we have analyzed in this work.

Desdemona is the typical adolescent of our times—impulsive and ahead in her beliefs. She is rebellious and decides to do exactly the opposite of what her father thinks she should do, she must do, or is the best for her. In doing what she desires, she meets a perverse Iago, whose envy, malevolence, hatred, and ambitions induce her loving husband, Othello, to murder her. Shakespeare created stereotypes in this play, but they have come to be accepted. The perceptions of women and men and the way people made judgments about others were also defined in this work. We think that the blackness of Othello is not the real cause of the tragedy. The main tragedy here, besides Iago's intrigues, is the fact that Desdemona did not become aware of the change in her husband, of his altered perception about her, in time, and thus she accepted in silence, with resignation, her destiny almost with a religious devotion.

Her moral law of life and ambitions are the essential substances that are also present in the final tragedy of Lady Macbeth. The story is an account of how a human being can be pushed into the abyss because of her memories, defect of imagination, and excess of propensity to act. The play itself is a vivid evocation of an infernal relationship with nature, night, and evil. Lady Macbeth is touched by this evil perversity, and we see how she lights the sinister forces in her husband, who cannot stop once he commits the first crime. The morality theme of crime and punishment works out perfectly in this story. In her sleepwalking scene, we see the horror of the murders, the infernal sufferings of the criminals, the way a murder comes to light sooner or later, and the psychic forces that are gnawing at Lady Macbeth up to the end of her life.

Cleopatra is definitely another type of woman. She did some deeds of ingenuousness like the young Desdemona, but she also showed something of the ambitiousness of Lady Macbeth, with the significant difference that Cleopatra worked herself toward her own death scene, like a fictional masterpiece that transcends a normal fiction of tragedy and becomes reality. After the greatness of her reign, she is a mere parody of a queen. And Antony, who meant many things to her, deserted everything in his life—as a Roman, as a soldier, and as the ruler of a third of the world—for her love. This made it imperative that Cleopatra should die in the way she did: beautifully, serenely, peacefully, ostentatiously, with her crown and garments, as a tragic queen.

Language is very important to connect audiences and readers, and it is a main force in these plays. Its verbal richness, the abundance of details about the characters, and the coverage of various topics give us a clear idea not only of historical and political events but also of geography, animals, and customs of the times in which these people lived.

We can say also that there are some biblical

implications in the works of the great Shakespeare, especially in the sense of how much we can learn from the characters of his plays. Bad and good are present in most of them. We can see paradise for those who behave well and hell for those whose acts deserve to be punished. How we judge each character's behavior depends on our moral or religious formation. But we must remember that Shakespeare did not write about them to give us the opportunity to do psychological analyses of the characters; he just wrote for performance.

Bibliography

Bamber, Linda. *Comic Women, Tragic Men*.
Board of Trustees of the Leland Stanford
Junior University. Stanford, CA: Stanford
University Press, 1982.

Bevington, David, ed. *The Bantam
Shakespeare: Macbeth*. New York: Bantam
Books, 1988.

Bloom, Harold. Comp., *Modern Critical
Interpretations of William Shakespeare's
Antony and Cleopatra.* New York: Chelsea
House, 1988.

———. *Modern Critical Interpretations of
William Shakespeare's Macbeth.* New
York: Chelsea House, 1987.

Bradley, A. C. *Shakespearean Tragedy
Lectures on Macbeth.* London: McMillan
and Co., Ltd. 1919.

Colie, Rosalie. *Shakespeare's Living Art*. New Jersey: Princeton University Press, 1974.

Doyle, John, and Ray Lischner. *Shakespeare for Dummies*. New York: IDG Books Worldwide, Inc., 1999.

Foakes, R. A. *The Applause Shakespeare Library: Macbeth*. New York: Applause Books, 1996.

Gaines, Barry, ed. *The Applause Shakespeare Library: Antony and Cleopatra.* New York: Applause Books, 2001.

Garfield, Leon. *Shakespeare Stories*. New York: Schoken Books, 1995.

Gray, John. *Men, Women and Relationships*. New York: Harper Paperbacks, 1996.

"Greek Tragedy." Retrieved 2004–2014 from http://www.bsu.edu/classes/magrath/cc201ss/tragedy/GreekTragedy.html.

Lamb, Sydney, ed. *Cliffs Complete: Shakespeare's Othello*. New York: IDG Books, 2000.

Lee, Boltin. *Cleopatra VII: Last Pharaoh of Egypt*. Chicago: 2002. http://www.Royalty.nu/Africa/Egypt/Cleopatra.html.

"List of Creation Myths." Wikipedia.org. Retrieved 2009–2014 from http://en.wikipedia.org/wiki/List_of_creation_myths.

Maurer, Kate, ed. *Cliffs Complete: Shakespeare's Othello*. New York: IDG Books, 2000.

Mowat, Barbara, and Paul Werstein, ed. *The New Folger Library: Shakespeare, Antony and Cleopatra*. New York: Washington Square Press, 1999.

———. *The New Folger Library: Shakespeare, Othello*. New York: Washington Square Press, 1999.

Muir, Kenneth, ed. *The Arden Shakespeare: Macbeth*. Zagreb, Croatia: Thomas Nelson and Sons, 1984.

Onions, C. T. *A Shakespeare Glossary*. New York: Oxford University Press, 1986.

"Otelo, el moro de Venecia" [Othello, the Moor of Venice], Biografias & Vidas [Biographies and Lives]. Retrieved 2009–2014 from http://www.biografiasyvidas.com/monografia/shakespeare/otelo.htm.

Pickett, Joseph P., ed. *The American Heritage Dictionary of the English Language,* 4th ed. New York: Random House Inc., 2001.

Rogers, Pat (2006), Johnson, Samuel (1709–1784), *Oxford Dictionary of National Biography* (online ed.), Oxford University Press, retrieved August 25, 2008, from http://www.conservapedia.com/Samuel_ Johnson.

Russell Brown, John, ed. *The Applause Shakespeare Library: Othello.* New York: Applause Books, 2001.

Salgado, Gamini, and Fenella Salgado. *Shakespeare's "Othello" (Critical Studies).* UK: Penguin Books Ltd., 1989.

Williams, Edwin B., ed. *The Bantam New College Spanish & English Dictionary.* Rev. ed. New York: Bantam Books, 1999.

Printed in the United States
By Bookmasters